Growing Into God

A scientist's perspective on faith,
the universe and why I believe in
God

by

Dr Tobias Thornes

WASH HOUSE PUBLISHING

Non-fiction

Published by Wash House Publishing 2020

Printed on demand by CPI Group.
The CPI Group is committed to the prevention of
pollution and continual improvement to reduce our
effect on the environment.

ISBN 9781787234697

About the Author

Dr Tobias Thornes is a Christian, scientist and writer. He studied Physics & Astronomy at the University of Durham, before obtaining a DPhil in Atmospheric Physics at the University of Oxford. He is at the time of writing in discernment for vocation in the Church of England. He has written numerous articles, papers and books on topics ranging from physics and environmental science to poetry and economics. His recent publications include:

The Problem with Money: Towards a New Economics (2018)
The Problem with Money: Solving the Problem (2019)
Requiem for the Intercity 125: Poems of Travel and Change (2019)

To Nathan

He that believeth in me, though he were dead, yet shall he live: and whoso liveth and believeth in me shall never die.

John 11:25-26

Contents

Foreword

In an age where science and technology are in a state of unprecedented progress, and amidst the busyness of modern-day life, there can sometimes be little time for spiritual reflection. When religious institutions such as the Church have come to outsiders to seem old-fashioned or even anachronistic, set against the newness of a twenty-first century culture of innovation, it is all too easy to believe the fallacy that 'science' and 'religion' are polar opposites. There are some prominent voices who will tell you that the former is all enlightenment and the latter mere superstition; that the former is the Truth and the latter no more than a bundle of lies and fancies.

It seems a fitting time, then, to make the case that the reality is quite different. When these terms are interpreted accurately, it becomes clear that science is a religious activity; religion is a scientific endeavour. Both involve the search for Truth and meaning in our lives; both require us to have faith of some sort – whether it's in ourselves, in others, in particular methods we use, or in God.

I wrote this book, *Growing into God*, in an attempt to provide a scientist's perspective on God, creation, and on what is truly meaningful in our lives. Partly, the book is a direct response to *Outgrowing God*, a 2019 work in which Richard Dawkins lays out an argument against the existence of God from his own perspective as an atheist scientist, and I would like to acknowledge and thank him for his book. The science of *Outgrowing God* is impeccable, but I hold that the philosophical conclusions he draws from it are flawed. Readers of both books may notice some similarity in the approach taken, and I have tried to respond to all the points that he made in his book, and explain why I – as a physical scientist – disagree with many of his assertions and misrepresentations of theism.

However, I do not explicitly mention either *Outgrowing God* or Professor Dawkins in what follows, and *Growing into God* is intended to be read as a stand-alone volume. Its aim is to set out why all the evidence at my disposal convinces me that God does indeed exist, is present in our lives, and calls us into relationship with Him. The title *Growing into God* is not accidental; It is my contention that the whole of our lives involves growing in our understanding of and relationship with God. Far from 'growing out' of our belief in God as we age, the more we learn of life and the universe we live in, the clearer our vision of Him becomes.

This book is, inevitably, written from the perspective of a Christian scientist, because that's what I am, but I hope that you will enjoy it and gain something from it whatever your faith, or even if you do not believe in God. If it convinces you at least not to dismiss outright the idea of there being scientifically sound evidence in favour of God's presence, my aim will have been accomplished. Although I am a member of the Church of England, the views I express here may not always accord with those of other Christians (or theists) on all points, and should be taken as my own.

Foreword

I would like to thank the various people of many faiths – and none – who have contributed to this book by reading preliminary chapters and providing their helpful comments: my agnostic brother Gabriel, who checked my biology in chapter 8; Professor Ifan Hughes, who brought his expertise in quantum mechanics to check my working in chapter 9; and my one-time chaplain at Oriel College, Oxford and friend Revd Robert Wainwright, whose help with the theology of Chapters 2 and 3 was invaluable.

This book is dedicated to my dear departed friend Nathan John, without whose inspiration, enthusiasm and Christian support I would not be where I am now.

Tobias Thornes
Hadzor
May 2020

Part One

Waking up to God

1

Many gods?

Do you believe in God?

I don't ask 'do you believe in *a* god?' – in this god, or that god, in any object or person that has been or is still worshipped as 'a god'. No: in this book, I'm asking whether you believe in God with a capital 'G', and I think you know what I mean.

I mean The God, the One God, the God who made everything, who knows everything, who joins together the loose strands of this sometimes confusing and varied universe into one coherent whole. The God who made the universe. The God who speaks to you in countless signs in the world around you, in numerous 'coincidences', in a helping hand just at the time you need it, in the kind words of a neighbour. The God that is within everything, with you always, who knows your inmost thoughts and your deepest dreams. This is the God of all the world's faiths that are known as 'monotheistic' – that is, the faiths that worship the One God who is everything, not many gods. He is the Jewish Yahweh, the Muslim Allah, the Christian God.

And He is an entirely different reality from the concept of a 'god' that is one among many. There have been many 'polytheistic' or 'many-god' religions over the course of human history, though most are now extinct or have very few followers (Hinduism is sometimes called a polytheistic religion, but many Hindus are in fact monotheists, as they believe in one God in many forms). Why did these religions come to be? All religions are an attempt to make sense of life, and these religions arose spontaneously across all parts of the world because of a primitive human desire to establish meaning and purpose in the world – a desire that has drawn later human beings, in their billions, to the worship of God.

A 'god' with a small 'g' is really nothing other than a person: it is some being that has, or is perceived to have, rational agency. The gods that polytheists worship might be actual people, like Roman emperors or celebrities in our own time; they might be imaginary people, like the Viking gods Odin and Thor or the Egyptian Osiris and Horus, amongst countless others that people have dreamed up; or they might be animals or objects – trees, stars, pieces of wood or stone – that polytheists treated as if they had autonomy and consciousness. The worship of such gods originated in human beings' interactions with one another, and our own ignorance of the distinction between real people and inanimate objects. After all, millennia before modern science, who was to say that the Sun, or a tree, or a river, say, didn't have a 'spirit' that could listen to us and respond to us like a human being might? Nearly all 'gods' originated in physical objects or dead people that human communities decided that they ought to worship.

Why? Because of what they thought they could get from these gods in return. If you're nice to a human, you expect them to be nice to you back. So, in a situation where you don't know whether the weather will be good or bad and you're worried about the harvest being good enough to last you through the winter, you're fearful that plague will break out, or dread that an enemy kingdom might attack you, defeat you and steal all you have, why not pray to the 'gods' for protection?

If you prayed to the Sun, the logic went, she might give you good weather for the harvest. Pray to a tree and he will bless you with fruit, pray to the river and she will flood at the right time to fertilise the soil. Pray to a planet and it could influence your good or bad fortune – Mars, for instance, might aid you in war. All, that is, as long as you please these gods and give them the sacrifices they desire. If things go wrong, it must be because you've fallen short or displeased them somehow. Such was the notion behind the numerous 'gods' of the polytheistic ancient world.

I don't believe in any such gods. I don't believe in a 'god' of this kind at all. But I do believe in God. God is fundamentally different from these other 'gods' because God isn't to be found in a rock or a tree or a wandering star. He isn't a mythological person of whom we tell tales to explain how the world is – a giant who dropped a hammer to form an island or any such superstition. God wasn't invented by human beings at all, not even as an explanation cooked up to plug a gap in our knowledge about something we didn't understand. God is everything. That's why there can only be one of him – he's left no room for anything else! The monotheistic God is within us and without us, and to worship any of the polytheistic gods is to deny this – to venerate individual parts of him independently of him – and thus to deny the Truth in the monotheist's mind.

To deny the truth is what we call 'blasphemy'. This has become a bit of a dirty word since it was used by a corrupt medieval church to control and cajole people, but it's really just a synonym for falsehood. Just as to deny the truth that the world is round is a blasphemy against geography, so to deny that God is One is a blasphemy against God. It's simply not true. But one who's never learnt Geography can't be blamed for their blasphemy about the shape of the Earth, and nor can anybody who's never been told the truth about God be blamed for not knowing it!

Some people say that Islam and Christianity are really polytheistic, because Muslims and Christians believe in 'the Devil' – 'Lucifer' or 'Satan' he's sometimes called, 'Shaytan' in Islam. This is to fall foul of a gross misunderstanding. In truth, Lucifer is not a separate god from God: God is in everything, there is nothing else. What Lucifer represents is a 'fallen angel': a part of God that rebels against God's will. We all have parts of ourselves that rebel against out better judgement, and the same is true of God and his creation as a whole. This rebellious part of God is in all of us. It's what causes us to deny his existence and his will, to do bad things to him and to one another, given that we are all part of him. An 'angel' is just a fancy word for a rational agent – a human being, say – who does God's will, whereas a 'devil' is one who subverts it, who 'sins'. We all have both angelic and devilish parts to our personalities. We'll come on to why God might allow part of himself to subvert his own will later, but for now think of it as being like a hand or a foot that doesn't do what you want it to, but spasms out of control. It's still part of the same body; we're all part of the one God and so is that part of each of us that is 'devilish'. Muslims and Christians do not believe in a devil 'god'; they are not polytheists.

Now, at this point I have a confession to make. I am not by training a theologian, so I can't quote to you reams of theological texts and commentaries to back up what I say. I am a scientist – a physicist, to be specific – so my evidence comes from my senses and experiences, observation and experiment, as well as what I read of others' learning. As a scientist, I'm interested in the truth, and in evidence for what is true. I'm not interested in any mumbo-jumbo superstition that doesn't stand up to scientific scrutiny.

We have no evidence to believe in the many gods of the polytheistic religions, as far as I can tell, and no evidence that praying to Mars will help you win a violent battle, or that sacrificing a goat to the god of rain will ensure he keeps his clouds away for your holidays. There's no more evidence to believe in such gods than there is to believe in fairies, or pixies, or chocolate teapots in orbit around the Sun for that matter. I've never met anyone who truly believed that there is a teapot of any kind in a lone orbit around the sun, nor come to think of it have I met anyone – so far as I can tell – who genuinely believes in fairies. Not even my five-year-old niece. She'll make-believe for a while, but she knows that no such thing really exists. Of course she does – her parents are scientists too! And Muslims. They're interested in the truth, interested in God – not in made-up gods and not in fairies. They will have told her that God is real, and that fairies are not.

And why shouldn't they? You would tell your daughter that the stove is hot, since you know it to be true and want to protect her by sharing this truth with her. She'd find out for herself soon enough, but it's easier and less painful for her if you tell her before she gets herself burnt. She might not listen to you; she might end up learning 'the hard way', but you'd want to warn her all the same. The same is all the more true of God, the most important truth anyone could ever know. God isn't some abstract concept – like the alphabet or the numbers we use to count things with – that humans have invented. He's as real and physical as the heat of the stove, and any good parent would want to tell their children about such things, to help them, to stop them getting hurt. All human knowledge and progress depends upon our passing on truths to one another.

If you can tell a child that pixies aren't real, why shouldn't you tell her that God is? It will help her to conceptualise what she may already feel inside her. That's not to say that parents have to tell their children about God in order for the children to believe in him, as if he were some secret tradition known only to a few. God can reveal himself however he wishes. But why wouldn't they? Why wouldn't they share the best news they've ever heard with those they love the most?

I'm not arguing here that children should be somehow indoctrinated into religion – whether that's theistic religion, or indeed atheism – or told what to think. My religion, Christianity, is all about seeing for yourself, thinking for yourself, meeting God for yourself, albeit alongside and with the support of millions of other believers. Children should be shown truths and taught facts, but allowed to think howsoever they please. That's what God intended – otherwise he wouldn't have made us rational agents capable of free thought, and even of going against his will, in the first place! If God doesn't force us to believe in him, how could it possibly be right for us to force one another? It cannot.

A child may be baptised, circumcised, or undergo an initiation ritual. There's no harm (and sometimes there's a lot of good) in that. But they are never really a Christian, a Jew, a Muslim, an atheist, a pagan, or whatever other religious label people may give them, until they are old enough to think for themselves, to see the evidence for themselves, to know God – or ignore him – for themselves. They must be able to choose to follow Christ, obey the covenant, submit to the will of Allah (God), or not. That's what 'Christian', 'Jew' and 'Muslim' really mean.

Myself, I am a Christian because I have chosen to be one, following my heart, my mind and the evidence of all my senses. I was never 'made' to be a Christian by my parents, teachers or anyone else, though of course they introduced me to the Church. My brothers had the same parents and teachers. One of them is a devout Muslim, the other is a sceptical agnostic – the sort that believes there probably is no God, not the sort who thinks it's a 50-50 toss-up with no evidence either way. 'Agnostic' just means 'don't know for sure', but I suppose none of us really knows anything with absolute certainty, except the fact that something must exist, even if we ourselves, the world and the whole of space and time are mere illusions. Something is doing something, because I'm experiencing existence. We can only tell anything else based on the evidence we've got, and the evidence convinces me that there is a God.

We'll go more into the meat of this later, but suffice it here for me to rehearse a few things that make me convinced of God, despite not having any belief at all in gods, fairies, pixies, leprechauns, ghosts and messages in entrails (if you don't know, don't ask!). Firstly, billions of people in the world today believe in God, and a sizeable and growing percentage of the global human population have believed in God for many centuries, since Christianity hit the mainstream following the Emperor Constantine's conversion of the Roman Empire in 312 AD. None of those pagan 'gods' ever had so many adherents, even proportionally speaking. There are 1.9 billion Muslims, and 2.4 billion Christians, in the world, making up more than half of the global human population. Isn't it unlikely that so many people should all agree in their belief in God, giving up belief in gods and other superstitions, if there were nothing in it?

Incidentally, don't get put off by the fact that there are Roman Catholics, Anglicans, Protestants, Jews, Muslims and more making up the monotheistic religions of the world. All the monotheists worship the same God

- the creator of the universe - in different ways, and all agree in the fundamentals of loving him and one another. There are deep theological differences between some of them, but these relate more to how God has revealed himself to different people, and the different things he calls different groups of people to do, rather than to differences in beliefs about the nature of God himself. I believe that all are true, but that one is a fuller truth than all the others. But all worship of God - under whatever label - is pleasing to God if it is true worship, based upon love freely given. The specifics (church on a Sunday, pilgrimage to Mecca and so on) tend to be manmade traditions, are different for different groups with different needs, and aren't so important to him.

Christianity has been called polytheistic by those who do not fully understand it, because of the idea it espouses of the Trinity: Father, Son and Holy Ghost. But these are no more separate gods than 'heads' and 'tails' are different coins: they are three faces of the same thing, God. We often refer to this God as 'he' by convention - it's another of those unimportant human traditions - but you can call God 'she' or 'it' or whatever you like really, so long as you acknowledge the truth that God is One, the supreme being. He is not a person or object. He is God, and there is no definition we can give to completely describe him, other than God. Muslims have 99 names for him, and even these don't capture the fullness of his essence by a long way!

In the Biblical tradition that Jews and Christians follow, God defines himself as 'I am' - in other words, that which exists. But we can describe aspects of him: he is a creator, sustainer, friend, lover even. For this reason, Christianity chooses to focus on three aspects of God (confusingly called 'persons' by some, but they're not separate people!): not to split him into three gods but to emphasise his oneness, at the same time as elucidating the Truth about who he is from our viewpoint.

The Church has done a very bad job of communicating to people what the Trinity means, at least in recent years, making Christianity seem more confusing rather than revealing the simple truth. So, here is that truth – what the Trinity means. The Trinity is nothing more than a human way of visualising God's profound oneness: it's supposed to make him more accessible, not harder to understand! The fact is that God is so fundamentally One that he is at once a Father, Son and Spirit – all at the same time. This means that the God who created everything, watches over the universe and loves us and guides us like a father would (the Father) is the same One God who experiences our human existence every day (the Son), most perfectly manifested in Jesus Christ, who was the only human ever to be all angel and no devil (he didn't go against God's will at all), but also present inside all of us. And this is the same God whom we feel within ourselves and talk with when we pray, who inspires us through our lives and inspired the prophets to write the scriptures (the Spirit, or Ghost in old-fashioned language, again with a capital 'G' as he's not some sort of ethereal ghoul).

God is all three. It's like my dad. He's the son of my grandad, and he's also the father of me. And he is (alas) a supporter of Huddersfield Town football club.

The fact that he's one of these things doesn't preclude him from being either of the others. The father isn't a different person to the son, and he's not a different entity when he's shouting in disbelief and sorrow at yet another loss for his team. He's still my dad: all three in one and one in all three, and countless others besides – just as God can be described as countless other things than 'Father', 'Son' and 'Holy Ghost', though these are the three most encompassing terms.

The Trinity must be a human conception of God, because all numbers are human inventions, except one: the number One. Everything is fundamentally One, a truth that has been arrived at by countless people even outside the monotheistic faiths, from Buddhists to Big Bang scientists. All agree, although they are many and varied, in this. So in presenting further evidence for God, I could look to all sorts of scriptures and fulfilled prophecies, reported miracles and wonders of the world. Indeed, we'll look at many of these in the later chapters of this book. But my greatest piece of evidence comes from the Holy Spirit, from within myself.

I know with my inmost, deepest sense – a sense that I trust more surely than my eyes, more surely than my ears, than the touch of my hands and the taste of my tongue – that God is there. If I was blinded, deafened, relieved of my limbs and had my tongue cut out, I would still know that God was there. I feel his presence, listening to me. But I also see signs in the world all around me that represent him speaking back to me: coincidences that make the road he's set me on lead unexpectedly to good places, chance happenings and conversations that lead me where he wants me to go, occurring too often by far to have happened at random. I've studied statistics. I know this to be true. And when I let my mind wander towards the beginning of existence – the impossibility of anything existing at all, with nothing to precede it, I feel a terror within my very heart and soul. A terror of the void, which can only be filled by God.

Now, some people would reject this 'subjective' sort of evidence because it can't be objectively measured – nobody can verify my relationship to God with any kind of scientific instrument. But just because something isn't clearly visible to everyone – like the Sun, say – doesn't mean that that something isn't real. We all have faith in all sorts of things that we can't see or hear or physically touch for ourselves, but which others have assured us do exist. I've never seen the Sahara desert, or the Arctic, or the Taj Mahal – but I don't for a moment doubt they exist. To be fair, the existence of those places is accepted as an 'objective' fact because in principle anyone could go to those coordinates and verify that they do exist, and weren't just made up. But we all experience many things on a daily basis that can't be objectively verified in the same way. Indeed, all our relationships are characterised by subjective feelings that we can't scientifically 'measure' at all. I dearly love my border collie Blue, and I know that my love for him, and his for me, is very real – but nobody else can experience it. You too will have experienced love for individuals that are special to you, a love that nobody else shares. So it is with our relationship with God – it is a personal relationship, and is different for each of us. It can't be objectively measured, but that doesn't mean it isn't real.

Nobody believes in God because of scriptures. Scriptures like the Bible and Qur'an merely help us to build on the belief we already have and to learn to listen to his will, as well as offering us guidance in times of difficulty. We believe in God because we encounter him – in the Creation, in Christ, in our own hearts – and he speaks to our inmost selves. It is evident that not everybody possesses this sense of God's presence. Perhaps some people need more promptings – scriptures, yes, but also the help of others – to sensitise them to it. Some people, after all, are naturally tall, others short; some are naturally thin, others fat. Why shouldn't some be more naturally attuned to and aware of God, and others less so? In former ages, when diets were less nutritious, nearly everyone was short, thin and believed in God. They believed presumably because of environmental effects such as hardship, the need for help amidst a lot of desperation and the desire for comfort amidst the everyday reality of death. Such environmental influences can trump genetic dispositions in the same way that a shortage of food trumps a genetic disposition towards a large and healthy body. In today's world, there is an abundance of food and many of the dangers of life have been alleviated, so it is not surprising that people are less likely to be short and thin, and don't necessarily feel that they need God's help and protection as much.

Although subscription to organised religions such as Christianity has declined in recent decades, furthermore, this is not necessarily indicative of a declining sense of God. Very few people own the term 'atheist' (presumably partly because of cultural connotations associated with the word, which was once an insult) and many possess a belief in 'something beyond' the material world around us, sometimes believing in a 'deistic' God (one who made the universe, but has no ongoing personal relationship with us) or ascribing agency to the universe itself. Most people have a sense of purpose in their lives, and a sense of what is right and wrong, and many scientists are fascinated by the mystery of things beyond our understanding – Albert Einstein not least among them. All these people may betray an innate sense of God which, by failing to acknowledge him explicitly, they fail to develop into a concrete belief in him.

In any case, few of us (if any) sense God strongly enough to know what he wants us to do without any help from signs that he gives us in the world around us and in the testimony of others. One such source of understanding is a well-known library of books, each describing humanity's experiences of God at some time and place or another. This collection is known as the Bible (from the Greek for 'library'), and we shall explore what it can and cannot tell us in the next chapter. Another source is the lives and words of other people of faith who may have lived many years before us but have left an example to us, or whom we have known in our own lives and who have inspired us. Everybody knows people – past or present – who are inspirational in some way. In science we might be inspired by Charles Darwin, and his ability to put his finger on a beautiful biological truth that so many other people had missed; in art, perhaps Pablo Picasso, or Edward Elgar in music. Those particular people who are inspirational in the realm of faith are known as 'saints' in the Christian Church (other faiths have other terms).

Saints are not perfect people, and are certainly not gods (though certain sects of Christians have been accused of worshipping saints as if they were gods by other Christians, especially during the Reformation era when the issue led to great arguments within the Church). Saints are 'venerated', which is to say that they are remembered fondly for some aspect of how they lived or what they did or said. They are held up as a good example to us all. All deceased Christians are 'saints', but some are remembered especially because their lives show us something especially important. Roman Catholics are sometimes heard to pray to particular saints. But that is not because they think of the saints as somehow separate gods, but because they recognise that these saints, in doing the will of God, are in spirit as well as physically one with God. So praying to a saint is really the same thing as praying to God. A saint is never worshipped – that would be idolatry – but that doesn't mean they, as aspects of God, can't be petitioned.

Then why not pray to God directly? Well, all Christians do. But some people find it helpful to pray also to saints, to remind them that God is 'son' as well as 'father', with us in all the stresses, strains and messiness of everyday life. Praying to someone who, though now one with God in their death and resurrection in heaven, in life endured the same sorts of struggles as us but remained faithful to God, can be a great help, comfort and encouragement. That's why there are also such things as 'patron saints' associated with activities or places (the patron saint of Ireland is St Patrick, the patron saint of fishing is St Andrew) – such saints are reminders of people who lived and worked in the same places as we do, or did the same things as we do before us, and lived Christian lives.

Again, I emphasise that to monotheists there is only one God, but these saints all have their being in him. There have been many gods worshipped by people across the world for millennia, which have been forgotten entirely or at least abandoned by nearly everyone. They are a completely different sort of thing to the one true God worshipped by the vast majority of theists – indeed by the majority of people in the world today. He has revealed himself in many ways to many people, so that there now exist Muslims, Christians, Jews, Sikhs, Hindus and others all worshipping him. So many independent realisations that the universe is fundamentally united in one being, God, and that there are not many gods but only him, is very good evidence indeed that he not only exists, but has revealed his nature to many different peoples. It's taken humanity a while to work it out – our theological understanding has increased over time, just as our scientific and technological understanding has – but now we know the truth. Not many gods, but one God.

2

What is Truth?

'What is Truth?' This question, which according to the Biblical Gospel of John was asked of Christ by the Roman governor Pontius Pilate, resonates as much for us today as it would have done for people living at the time of Jesus Christ, some two thousand years ago. We are, as human beings, always seeking for understanding, and with our better parts seeking to know 'the Truth' about the world in which we live, our place in it, and why we are here in the first place.

Pilate's question comes after Jesus has told him, under interrogation by the governor, that he (Jesus) was 'sent into the world' in order to 'testify to the Truth'. In other words, Jesus is saying that he possesses the 'Truth' that we all yearn to know: in his words and in his deeds, he is able to reveal to those who look and listen the secret of 'life, the universe and everything' – to use a more contemporary phrase – which is to say, why we are here, what we ought to do with our lives, and what will come next. Indeed, John is careful in his Gospel to describe how Jesus represents the unravelling of a mystery, the revealing of a truth, that has been kept secret since the world began: the very meaning of life itself.

That's a bold claim. Naturally, if we believe it we should be eager to learn about what Jesus did and said, to find out for ourselves what is this 'truth' revealed to a carpenter from Galilee all that time ago. The 'New Testament' is a collection of books and letters written after the time of Jesus Christ (i.e. in the years AD), officially adopted by the Christian Church at the council of Nicaea in 325 AD, in order to recount these words and deeds to future Christians, alongside other wise words of the earliest followers of Jesus.

The New Testament is not, and was never intended to be, standalone proof of the existence of God or even of the existence of Jesus. For the latter, we could look to historical documents such as that of the Roman historian Tacitus, who wrote about Christians in Rome during the reign of the Emperor Nero (37-87 AD), describing them as an errant (and dangerous) sect among many others. He speaks of one called 'Christ' who was crucified by the governor Pontius Pilatus in Judea (the ancient home of the Jews). We can also look to subsequent events for evidence: the steady growth of Christianity from a small group of believers to a world-wide faith with billions of adherents. Even if they were mistaken about who he was, such a stalwart initial group branching out into such large eventual following leaves little doubt that Jesus existed. For proof of the existence of God, meanwhile – and of the veracity of Jesus' claims to be the Son of God – we need to look not to scriptures but to our own lives, our own experiences, and the life of the world around us. It is there that we see, hear, feel, touch and taste God's existence. More on this in later chapters. For now, though, let us focus on what the Bible can tell us, given that it's been so central in shaping many theists' beliefs about who God is.

With any historical document, it is vital that one bears in mind its purpose, and the intentions and possible biases of its author or authors before interpreting it. Very few Christians (or others for that matter) believe the Bible to be the literal word of God or its authors to have been infallible messengers from God. For the Christian, Christ (and what he said) is the Word of God – the actual 'truth' made flesh and blood – and he didn't write any of it. Rather, the Bible is a collection of accounts by human authors of their own and others' experiences of God. For Christians, those authors were inspired by God, which is what gives the text its veracity, but what they wrote wasn't dictated word by word by God, so it isn't necessarily complete or infallible. These experiences were written down not to record historical facts (most of the books in the Bible are written in a style that is ill-suited to that purpose) but to teach someone who already believes in God about what God has revealed to us concerning himself, who we are as human beings in relation to him, and how he wants us to be.

Hence, we shouldn't expect the Bible to give us lots of exact dates and times, or even necessarily to relay events in chronological order. We needn't even be sure that the events recorded literally happened in the way in which they are said to have happened – only that they were perceived to have happened in this way. For example, events that seem incredible, such as John the Divine seeing Christ come down out of heaven and angels fighting with beasts and so on, are usually visions rather than actual historical events. If God the Almighty wants to reveal something to the human beings he has created, he can do so either physically or by showing us such visions, and I believe he does both: some miracles are physical, others psychological. It doesn't matter.

What does matter, though, is that what the Bible tells us about human experiences of God do really reflect what those experiences were. In the case of the New Testament, it is important for Christians reading the text that Jesus really did do the things and speak the words (not necessarily the exact words, but along the same lines) he is reported to have done and said. Exactly when or how he did and said them are not important either to the books' authors or to Christians today. The important question is, then, how can we know that the New Testament (we'll deal with the Old Testament in the next chapter) accurately portrays Jesus Christ's nature and message?

The short answer is, we can't. Not for certain – but then again we can't know with absolute certainty that the words written in any book are true. You can't even know with certainty when, where and by whom a book was written, unless you witnessed it being written yourself! Taken as they are, without any other evidence being considered, the New Testament texts are no more or less likely to be true than any other historical texts. Most of the New Testament books were written by authors we know very little about; some, such as the Epistle to the Hebrews, have no known author at all. The exception to this is St Paul, who wrote many of the other epistles: we do know a lot about him, mostly because of the many things he wrote and what we're told about him in the Acts of the Apostles, a kind of follow-on volume to the Gospel of Luke, and written by Luke. More on Paul later. His letters are the oldest books in the New Testament, and even they date from at the earliest fifteen years after the death of Christ.

The Gospels – the big four books that detail the life and ministry of Christ himself – are later still. Among them, Mark's Gospel is believed to be the oldest by most scholars, though Luke shows evidence of having heard eye-witness accounts of Jesus' life that the other writers didn't have access to, so his Gospel may have been compiled not long after this, drawing on Mark as one of many sources of information. Matthew is an embellishment of Mark, and John's Gospel is believed not to have been written before AD 90 or so, the latest of the four by far. We don't really know who Matthew, Mark, Luke or John were; some people have made educated guesses, assuming that Luke is the same as 'Luke the physician' mentioned by Paul, and that John the 'evangelist' who wrote the Gospel of John also wrote the three letters of John in the New Testament. But the truth is that we don't know, and it doesn't really matter that we don't know, from the Christian's perspective. That's because the writers were more interested in telling us about Jesus than about themselves.

Some people doubt that the accounts of the four Gospels are accurate portrayals of Jesus, for two main reasons. Firstly, they are written so long after the events they describe (at least thirty years, at most about seventy) that they must have been based on memories and rumours. Hence, it is argued that they are likely to have been subject to errors and embellishments that inevitably arise when stories are passed down orally between many people. Secondly, there are a few small discrepancies between the four. But neither of these lines of argument really constitutes any substantial evidence that the gospels are not true. Although it is true that they do not all contain the same events of Jesus' life – the raising from death of Lazarus, for instance, is only described in John's Gospel – they agree on all important theological points and very rarely explicitly contradict each other, if at all. Christ's teachings in all four complement one other; the vital story of Christ's arrest, trial, crucifixion and resurrection occur in all four.

Those areas where there are possible contradictions relate to smaller details that are not really important to the Christian, such as the lineage of Jesus' stepfather Joseph, which is recorded differently in Matthew and Luke. These differences largely stem from the different emphases the writers place on different aspects of the story, which in turn result from their differing interpretations of exactly what Jesus' life meant (so-called 'theological' differences), and their different audiences. Take Matthew, for instance. Matthew seems to have missed out a few generations in tracing the descendants of King David, and the longer line that Luke uses may differ because Luke's is not entirely male. The other gospels have Jesus crying out different words on the cross to those that Matthew uses, and it is quite possible that Matthew has altered a few minor details in his account in order to emphasise to his readers that Jesus is the Messiah prophesied in earlier writings. He has Jesus quote from psalm 22 on the cross, 'My God, my God, who have you forsaken me?' to draw our attention to that prophetic psalm. It is Matthew who emphasises the virginity of Jesus' mother Mary at the start, as a fulfilment of the ancient prophecy of Isaiah that a virgin would give birth to a son who would be called 'God with us'. That's because what Matthew in particular is interested in is not what Jesus' actual words were on the cross, or whether Mary's conception was really immaculate. Rather, believing Jesus to be the Messiah foretold by the prophets, he writes his account in a way that draws out the facets of Jesus' life that fulfil earlier scriptures. Matthew was, after all, writing for a Jewish audience so he wanted them to know that Jesus' life was foretold by Jewish prophecies.

The fact is that Jesus' death and resurrection and the events that surround it do closely match the words of psalm 22, written hundreds of years earlier, from 'they pierced my hands and my feet' (Jesus' hands and feet would have been pierced with nails when he was crucified) to 'they parted my garments among them' (all the gospel accounts record how the Roman soldiers cast lots for his clothing). Matthew draws attention to this by having Jesus quote the psalm. Since all the gospel writers are concerned more with Jesus' significance than with historical chronology, it is not at all surprising that they each bring a slightly different flavour to what they write, drawing out certain aspects of the story and perhaps occasionally fleshing out what they knew to have occurred in order to emphasise certain points that they considered important. The Bible is not a court testimonial or a witness statement. It is an authoritative guide to moral and theological truth.

Indeed, were the Gospels to have been written independently of one another, the similarity between them would have been remarkable. More likely, of course, is that they shared common sources or even inspired one another – parts of Matthew and Luke's gospels are almost identical to corresponding passages of Mark, and scholars have speculated that there was also another source, 'Q' common to both of them. John is very different in style to the others, and some of its sources may have been different – a different set of eye-witnesses that saw different events occur. Some people think that because all the gospels were written so long after Jesus' life, and their similarities could be a result of their simply copying one another, what they record is false. But the same argument would not readily be applied to a similar set of historical texts in another context. If we had four written records of the Battle of Hastings, each mostly in agreement but with slight variations, we wouldn't conclude that they all were false, the battle never happened, and any similarities were based on the authors copying one another. Many historical records – such as chronicles written by medieval monks – were written decades or centuries after some of the events they record; that's not usually on its own a reason for an historian to dismiss them.

What's different about the Gospels – and the reason why some people are so unwilling to believe their veracity – is that what they claim to have occurred is, on the face of it, incredible. Jesus is recorded performing many miracles, things that seem to be impossible and are not witnessed (at least, not by most of us) today: the sick are instantly·healed, the blind are cured, the dead are raised, Jesus himself is resurrected from the dead. Water is turned into wine in John's gospel; food is miraculously multiplied in all four. We could have a hundred gospels, even video footage if such a thing existed back then – some people would still believe it was fake, because things are happening that according to our everyday experience seem impossible.

But that doesn't mean than these miracles actually are impossible, from a scientific point of view. Indeed, science is all about carrying out experiments and making observations of the world to establish the truth and test our theories. Science can never tell us that something is impossible; only that in all our experiments and observations we've never seen it happen – which doesn't mean it can't happen if, for example, God comes to Earth in the form of a man or some other special circumstance. I believe that God created the universe and isn't bound by its laws and conventions: with God, nothing is impossible.

However, much like some branches of science (especially quantum physics), the Gospels do ask us to suspend our common sense, so we shouldn't blindly believe them without a second thought. The problem is compounded by the fact that that none of the Gospel writers witnessed any of this first-hand (except possibly John, but most Biblical scholars now think that this is very unlikely). They're all stories, rumours perhaps, passed down from mouth to mouth over several years. Perhaps the earliest Christians didn't see any need to write down what they'd all seen and knew to be true anyway. By the time anybody realised that these things needed to be recorded before all Jesus' contemporaries were dead, some people argue, surely the 'Chinese whispers' effect would have eaten into the truth, distorting the original tales into exaggeration and error just like a story passed down a long line of people in a children's game. And who's to say the original stories weren't made up in the first place?

Now, the 'Chinese whispers' effect is a real one, and does indeed lead to seemingly plausible stories arising out of an original 'truth' that are in fact fabrications, subjected to the enthusiasms and mis-hearings of all the people passing on the rumour. But it is not an effect that has much relevance here. The reason is that many of Jesus' miracles were (we are explicitly told in the Gospels) seen by a great many people. Hundreds saw the resurrected Jesus, St Paul tells us; thousands were miraculously fed by him when he preached in the desert; the blind and lame were cured in the Jewish Temple amidst the many worshipers and in full view of the hostile Jewish authorities. These authorities didn't deny his healing powers, didn't deny his miracles – either at the time according to the Gospel accounts, or later on when tales of what had gone on were being collated. Instead, they took issue with Jesus performing miracles because it was the Sabbath day, when they said he ought to be resting.

Any one of these people – especially the Jewish authorities who wanted to quash any notion that Jesus was the messiah – could have corrected or denied the swelling rumours surrounding the Galilean preacher, so false stories would struggle to be passed down from mouth to mouth as if they were true. Furthermore, the witnesses would have been there, still alive for many years after the events to stop the stories being corrupted like Chinese whispers. After all, Chinese whispers are distorted precisely because they are whispers, so nobody can hear one another clearly or correct others' mistakes. These stories about Jesus weren't whispers: they were shouted from the housetops! Why? Because they were incredible – and because they were true!

Furthermore, we need not assume that the gospel writers were stupid. When they wrote up the sayings, deeds and story of Jesus, they wouldn't have cobbled together any old gossip they found on the street. These were scholars who could write (unusual at the time), making cross-references to Old Testament scriptures and trying to interpret for themselves what Jesus meant. They weren't interested in half-forgotten fables: they were interested in the truth. They would surely have looked to the most reliable sources they could find to tell them about something so central to their faith – where possible, they would look to the witnesses of the events themselves, or those close to them. We know that Luke was a companion of St Paul (he tells us himself in Acts) and he knew personally some of the Apostles of Jesus, being amongst the earliest Christians. He seems to have interviewed Jesus' mother Mary or someone who knew her very well. Rumours of what happened didn't have to travel far to reach his pen. 'Chinese whispers' is not, therefore, something we need to worry about with him.

So the Gospels are very unlikely to have been much corrupted by the passage of time since Jesus lived. But what about the notion that the whole thing was completely made up, that the early Apostles, and the Gospel writers themselves, were elaborate liars peddling the equivalent of a first-century conspiracy theory? Well, if they were, it was a dangerous game to be playing. These people risked their very lives to spread the 'truth' about Jesus Christ. Many of them were martyred – arrested, mocked, even stoned to death – for what they were saying, for proclaiming that Jesus had risen from the dead. That message was just too much of a threat to the powerful. Would the first Christians really endure all this for something they knew to be a lie? It seems unlikely. And what a ridiculous thing to make up – that the Jewish Messiah, their king, had come as a poor, dirty carpenter from Nazareth who'd been arrested by a Roman lightweight, didn't lift a finger in his own defence and died the excruciating death of a common criminal, before miraculously coming back and disappearing again! All within living memory of the people they were telling this to.

It's not the most believable story; the evidence of the witnesses must have been rather good for it to catch on, and it's not the first thing you'd make up if you wanted to start a new movement for change. If one was to invent a Messiah, he would have to be a king like the kings of Israel of old, not this apparent failure. Yet somehow the story took off, and before long there were thousands, then millions, then billions of believers. The Roman Emperor himself abandoned his gods and converted, albeit nearly three centuries after the first Christians. We don't know all the details of what was happening in those early centuries, but we can still see the effects today.

It must have been a very powerful story indeed – much more powerful and widespread than any modern-day conspiracy theory. How many people in the world today really believe that the Moon landings were faked? That the September 11th 2001 attacks on New York were orchestrated by the USA itself? That there was a secret government cover-up of an alien visitation in 'Area 51'? Very few. Do we expect that conspiracy theories such as these, all of which have their adherents, will take off exponentially so that billions of people eventually believe them, even 2000 years hence? For the Moon landings to have been faked and the secret yet kept would have been miraculous, it seems so improbable when one surveys the evidence. The miracles Jesus is said to have done were even more miraculous – so, if they were completely untrue, how can they have inspired belief in so many millions or even billions of intelligent, rational people over the centuries?

It's true that there were many other travelling preachers in the region at around Jesus' time who inspired small followings. Why does nobody remember them today, or recount their supposed miracles? In all probability, there must have been something truly remarkable about Jesus Christ; even something divine about him. The four Gospel writers were clearly sufficiently overawed by him and his followers to pen such lengthy descriptions of his ministry. They weren't much interested in the first thirty years of his life (about which they could undoubtedly found out much more had they wanted to) – only his ministry, which began with Jesus' baptism at the age of thirty, and the signs that God then began working through him.

What's more, we don't only have the Gospel writers' word for it. St Paul was living as a Christian convert spreading the message of the Gospel far and wide, just a few years after Christ's crucifixion. He knew some of the Apostles chosen by Christ personally, including James and Peter, we are told in Luke's Acts of the Apostles. Paul was a reluctant convert to Christianity at first, a Jewish zealot who persecuted Christians as heretics and was quite happy to see them stoned to death. But after seeing a vision of Jesus himself (so Paul writes), he became the most ardent evangelist for the new movement, before the word 'Christian' had even been invented.

Paul wrote many letters to the churches he visited, some of which we still have today as part of the New Testament. By 'church', I don't mean a building, but a community of Christians. Incidentally, the Church (with a capital 'C') means the single worldwide community of Christians (though which denominations this includes depends upon who you ask). Most of what Paul wrote was advice to particular churches about what to do and how to act, with very little of the story of Jesus' life included. This is probably because Paul did his 'evangelising' – that is, converting people to Christianity – face-to-face, and he and his followers would already have shared the good news of Christ with all these people. His letters weren't intended to be gospels in and of themselves, but to give particular advice to particular people about particular issues that had arisen in Paul's absence. Most of the people Paul wrote to already knew about Jesus' life and sayings; it was how to implement a Christian way of living and preaching in their particular circumstances that they needed Paul's help with.

What Paul does tell us about Jesus' life, though, corroborates what the Gospel writers also say. In his first letter to the Corinthians (he wrote two surviving letters to the church in the city of Corinth), Paul describes the Last Supper Jesus had with his disciples, Jesus' death on the cross and his resurrection, and makes these the cornerstones of his faith. If Jesus wasn't resurrected, he points out, he can't have been who he claimed to be – the Son of God – because God wouldn't have just left his son to die in agony as the end of the story, and Christianity would be a red herring. If Christ was resurrected after death, though, God must have been with him, and what he taught (including that we are resurrected from death after we die) must be true. Remember that God loves truth, and hates falsehood and deceit. So does his Son.

Taking into account the four Gospel accounts, Paul's letters, the contemporary accounts by historians such as Tacitus and the effect that Jesus had – causing so much excitement for so many people – there can be little doubt to a scientific mind that Jesus existed, that his teachings were roughly what the Gospels say they were, and that he was crucified and resurrected. The sheer radical quality and consistency of his teachings, and his emphasis on universal love, are consistent with this being the true revelation of God, in accordance with all the other evidence we have about God (more on the morality of Christian teaching later). Whether Christ really was born of a virgin (as recounted in Matthew and Luke's Gospels), and which of the miracles he is said to have done literally happened as opposed to being metaphorical, has been and remains a matter of debate even amongst Christians. We can't know, and it doesn't really matter. What matters to Christians is that he is the Son of God, and what he with God's authority commands us: above all things to love one another. The miracles are all both a testimony to Jesus' identity, and an illustration of that love, shown by God towards all of us. The one miracle that really is important above all others for Christians is that of the resurrection. Whether you believe that Christ rose from the dead, and are willing to live on the basis of this belief, is what divides a Christian from a non-Christian: nothing more. I believe, having weighed up the evidence of ancient scriptures, other people's testimony, and the way in which my own heart and feelings are directed by God, that he did.

Let me justify that assertion. Why, exactly, do I believe Christ's resurrection? For three main reasons. Firstly, I trust the Gospel writers and St Paul. These were people inspired by Christ, preaching a way of life that was loving, forgiving, selfless and honest. They're not the sort of people one would expect to lie in such a flagrant and sophisticated manner. Nor were Jesus' closest followers, the Apostles, who would have been these writers' primary sources of information – and, as I've already mentioned, risked life and limb to spread the message of Christ. I don't think any of these people were infallible. I think the Gospel writers probably did mould the events they describe to fit their own interpretations of those events. Perhaps Matthew and Luke were wrong about Mary being a Virgin (I don't see any reason to believe that they were), over-excited by a prophecy of Isaiah written hundreds of years before in which the prophet speaks of a 'virgin' giving birth as a sign from God. Actually, the original Hebrew word for 'virgin' could also just mean 'young woman', but the context implies 'virgin' because Isaiah is clearly suggesting that something miraculous is going to happen at some point in the future. A young woman giving birth wouldn't be much of a sign, unless she was a virgin! Isaiah is clearly talking about events long after the lifetime of the people to whom he is speaking, because he says that Syria and Damascus (both great kingdoms in his time) will fall before the miraculous event takes place. The Gospel writers may or may not have been right about Mary, but I'm quite sure that they were spot on when it comes to who Jesus was and the meat of Jesus' message, which is what's most important.

Secondly, I trust God. For the reasons I explained in chapter 1, I know that he is there, that he exists, and that he guides me – and countless others – in our reading scripture. If the message that scripture gives us is wrong, I believe that he would have revealed this to us by now. As I said before, scripture is not evidence for the existence of God; it's the other way round. The fact that God exists is what gives scripture its veracity. To get the most out of it, the believer must trust him first, then read of these encounters between humans and the divine. The believer must interpret scripture in light of what they know about God already from their own and others' experiences of Him in the world around us (so-called 'natural theology'), and his overarching will for humankind. God's will is love, above all things.

Thirdly, and perhaps most importantly, the proof of the pudding is in the eating. When I live as Jesus commands in the Gospels – I do not say that I always succeed in my ambition to do so, but I try – and pray to God in the way that Jesus directs, things work out well. My life is spiritually and emotionally enriched, and so are the lives of those around me, whether or not we are physically or materially poor. The same is true of countless other Christians, now and in the past – the saints – who have wrought much good in the world and obtained fulfilment in their lives by virtue of living out the Gospel. Let me be clear: I don't think that things work out well as a 'reward' for doing God's will: God loves us the same, whatever we do. Nevertheless, it stands to reason that we feel better and do better if we live in harmony with the plans of the One God – who cares for everyone – than when we work against him.

Christians have also done very bad things in the past: this I do not deny. They have caused misery to others by trying to enrich themselves with money, goods and power – but this is precisely what the Gospels teach us not to do. Those 'Christians' have not lived up to the

Gospel, and indeed we all fail at times to live up to the Gospel, when we fail to love one another above all things, and this is what causes us to suffer. God still loves us when we do wrong, but we and others will nonetheless often suffer as a direct result of that wrong. Had we listened to God, we wouldn't have done it, and the suffering would have been averted.

To love another being is, the Gospels tell us, to be willing to lay down one's own pleasure, comfort and even life itself for the benefit of that other. Rich and power-hungry crusader Popes and crooked bishops of the Middle Ages, religious bigots of the Reformation-era conflicts when people were burnt on the stake for deviating from the official doctrines of the Church, and predatory priests of recent times who use the Church as a cloak for their sins did not obey the Gospel, nor adhere to its dearest and most important commands. We all fall short, some probably more than others, because of the temptations of this world.

By contrast, the people who have made it their life's work to genuinely live out the gospel as fully as humanly possible include St Francis, who lived a life of poverty, simplicity, prayer and humble service; and religious leaders such as Wulfstan of Worcester, who despite being bishop of Worcester and Archbishop of York died washing the feet of the poor on the streets. The truth of the Gospels is proven to us all, every day, in our own experience of life: live as Christ tells us in these texts, rather than merely pretending to do so for our own glorification and material wealth, and life achieves its fullest richness.

This is also, as it happens, how I know that Islam is also a religion that reflects the true word and will of God. Muslims may not believe exactly the same things as Christians, but on the most important things – especially venerating Jesus (whom Muslims hold to be an important prophet) and loving God and one another, which is Christ's and the Qur'an's greatest commandment – they are in agreement, and Muslims as well as Christians yield good 'fruits' (to use the Biblical metaphor) of faith, love and joy. These three things are what life is about! They are the ends for which monotheistic religions centred on God exist. Any religion that yields these three is good in God's eyes; a pretence at religion that is not loving, joyful or faithful is not good.

Another factor that makes some people suspicious of the Gospels is that, although there are four included in the New Testament, there were in reality many others written that weren't included in the Bible. Why not? It can at first seem an arbitrary choice: why take the Gospels of Matthew, Mark, Luke and John as 'truth' and reject all the rest? Some of these gospels contain quite miraculous or unpalatable things; if you reject those, don't you have to accept that all the gospels – including the Biblical four – are unreliable? Shouldn't it be all or nothing?

The four Gospels included in the New Testament were chosen in AD 325 – over 250 years after the earliest was written – by the Council of Nicaea. This was a meeting of knowledgeable and influential Christians convened by the Roman Emperor Constantine, who wanted to standardise his newly-adopted religion so that it could become the official religion of the Empire, something which required choosing which texts about Jesus and his teachings Christians should use the guide their own lives. There was also politics at play here, of course: Constantine wanted to be in charge of his new religion, and he wanted to make sure its adherents would obey him as well as the teachings of God. So did the council's decision have more to do with worldly power than the will of God?

I would say not. As a theist, I might argue that God was guiding the council as it made its decisions, since it was made up of Christian people who were attentive to his guidance, and that the correct texts were chosen to include in the Bible by divine inspiration. Yet I don't think that much inspiration beyond ordinary intelligence was needed when deciding on which Gospels to include (though one of the council's members was adamant that it was God's will there must be four), because all the other gospels that survive are quite obviously inferior to the canonical (a fancy word for 'officially sanctioned') ones, in one way or another. It's not that they're necessarily false, as such: they're just not as useful. They lack some of the features of the Big Four, and don't really add anything important. Let's briefly consider the main ones and verify that this is indeed the case. It's not difficult to get hold of them (or their surviving parts) if you want to read them for yourself.

The gospels of the Nazarenes, the Egyptians, the Hebrews and the Ebionites, as scholars now refer to them, are four of the gospels that missed out at Nicaea which do not survive intact for us to read today. We only know about them at all because of quotations from them that are found in other works. They appear to be narrative-style gospels (so, telling the story of Jesus), but they were all written later than the canonical four, and two of them seem to be based on Matthew, but doctored to fit the particular beliefs of the particular people who used them. The Hebrews one, for example, emphasises Jesus' Jewishness. They may have been useful at their time in the places that they served, but these gospels don't really add anything above what's already found in Matthew from the standpoint of the universal Church.

Then there's the Coptic Gospel of Thomas. This isn't a narrative, just a collection of Jesus' sayings, most of which can be found in the Big Four but are here without context, making this gospel less useful. It may even have been compiled using the canonical Gospels. The Gospel of Peter, meanwhile, is a narrative which takes a violently anti-Jewish line and which was already mired in controversy, with its authorship in doubt, before Nicaea. The Gospel of Mary only narrates events after Jesus' resurrection, whilst the Infancy Gospel of Thomas tells of Jesus' life as a child, claiming that he performed miracles, punished people he didn't like with death and raised them back to life. Neither of these tells us much about the core of Christ's message. The Gospel of Philip appears to be a set of out-of-context sermons that are difficult to interpret. The Proto-gospel of James (popular in the Middle Ages) is about the time before Jesus' birth; the Gospel of Truth is not specifically about

Jesus at all, just a long sermon about the nature of God; the Gospel of the Saviour is an embellishment of the account of the crucifixion that we have in the canonical Four.

The Epistle of the Apostles is an account of the Apostles talking with Jesus after the resurrection, whilst the Coptic Apocalypse of Peter is an account of Peter's visions – a bit like Revelation, but much shorter. The Second Treatise of the Great Seth is so opposed to Christian teaching – it implies that Christ stood and watched while someone else was crucified in his place – that it could never find a place in the canon. Finally, the Gospel of Judas is an apology for the betrayer of Christ.

Reading these gospels – or the fragments that remain – it is striking how less complete, less coherent and less useful they are than good-old Matthew, Mark, Luke and John with their much more comprehensive narratives interspersed with sayings of Jesus placed in the right context and forming an understandable picture. We must remember why the Biblical canon was being compiled in the first place: not as a random collection of anything that could be found about Jesus, but as a guide to moral and theological truth, a set of stories and letters that would illustrate to believers who Jesus was, but also what they should be, and what exactly his death and resurrection mean for us now. The four canonical Gospels – and the epistles – do this very well, taken as a whole. The other 'gospels', though what they say may in many cases be true and may sometimes be very interesting, do not.

It is important to acknowledge at this point that some of the things recorded in the Bible are according to our everyday experience impossible, and quite difficult to believe. Many of them are the subject of debate even amongst Christians: Christianity is after all a movement of intellectual curiosity, being grounded in a belief in Jesus Christ, through whom God came physically into the world to give us evidence of his love and his will. He showed us that he wants us to develop not a blind faith, but an evidence-based faith in him. That's why Christ appeared to 'doubting Thomas', we are told in the Gospel of St John, after the resurrection and allowed Thomas to touch his wounds to show that he really had died and been resurrected from the dead. It's that fact – the resurrection – that convinces me above all other evidence that Jesus was God in human form, and that his way is the way that God wants us to live. And it was proven to Thomas in flesh and blood.

We have already touched upon the Virgin birth as one source of controversy, given that Luke and Matthew trace Jesus' connection to King David through Joseph, then state that it wasn't Joseph but God himself who inseminated Mary. In that case, Christ is the Son of God – the highest King of all – so why should a connection to King David matter anyway? Well, it's very important in that it shows that the ancient Jewish prophecies have been fulfilled, and that God's promises have been kept. One can argue that Jesus was in Joseph's household, and by implication adopted into the 'House of David' as if he were 'born of David's line' – and God had promised David that he would always have a descendent on the throne of Judah. Jesus, as an everlasting king, fulfils that promise for all time. In Judaism, there was a lot of emphasis on blood – on the Jews being the chosen people by virtue of their biological bloodline. Christ – in his birth, as well as in his ministry – was opening up the Jewish inheritance to all people willing to believe in him: we can all be adopted as God's children, regardless of bloodline, just as Jesus was adopted by Joseph into the royal line of David.

Some have also cast doubt on Luke's account of Mary and Joseph going to Bethlehem for the birth because of a Roman census – why go to the city of David, if David was such a distant ancestor? Would Joseph even know what his ancestry was? Well, since David was the king – Israel's most famous king – it's likely that Joseph would have known that he was descended from him. Ancestry was a big thing in ancient Jewish culture. Anyway, for all we know, Joseph's father – or even Joseph himself – may have lived in Bethlehem before moving away not long before. Joseph may simply have been going back to his home town or place of birth to register. Luke was writing to a prominent Roman citizen, who would have known all about such censuses, so the idea of there being a Roman census in the region at around the time of Christ's birth must have been plausible. Luke wasn't out to make a fool of himself.

But these are mere practicalities. What of the miracles that Christ performed, according to the Gospels? Weren't these witnessed by thousands? On the other hand, don't they defy logic and physics? Take the 'feeding of the five thousand' recorded in all four

Gospels. Most Christians, like me, believe that Jesus really did multiply bread and fishes miraculously to feed that many – after all, God who is in all matter can do whatever he wants with it. Others believe it was merely symbolic, and that the 'miracle' Jesus performed was rather that of getting hard-hearted people to share with each other and bring out their hidden supplies. I won't get into the details of which is the better interpretation here, but the point is that Christians don't have to agree on what literally happened. Nor need we agree on whether the added stories in the Gospel of Matthew are true in the literal sense. His claims about the Jews crying out 'his blood be upon us and on our children' when Jesus was condemned to death, and the dead rising from their tombs after Jesus' resurrection (Matthew doesn't say they were seen before Jesus was resurrected, as some erroneously have claimed) – are designed to align with still more prophecies of the Old Testament that Jesus' ministry wouldn't be shown to fulfil without these stories.

Whether they literally occurred in the way they are described doesn't matter. The miracles may have really happened, they may have been visions or mass hallucinations according to your interpretation. But the message that Jesus was special, that he was God made man and that God loves us as his children – the message of true Christianity – that these miracles convey is the same. There's certainly nothing we can say about the veracity of the New Testament accounts that would be evidence against the existence of God or his love for humanity. Take them as metaphors or parables if you will, but that doesn't make them any less messages from God demonstrating the depths of his love for us and his power over the universe. The greatest miracle of all, still witnessed today, is that God is known by so many billions of Christians, Jews, Muslims and others, who all find that the Truth expressed in these texts aligns with their experience of the world. That, for me, is the greatest proof that the Torah, Gospels and Qur'an do indeed originate from God. How else could their influence spread so widely?

It must always be remembered that God can work in whatever way he wishes, an important consideration whether we're talking about modern-day miracles or scriptural ones. Take, for example, the vision at Fatima in Portugal in 1917, which is held by the Roman Catholic Church to have been a miracle. Seventy thousand people claimed to have seen the sun fall from heaven towards Earth, terrifying them for a terrible moment before resuming its usual place. This event had been foretold by the Virgin Mary to a young girl in a vision not long before, and it was the girl's report of this to the local people that led to such crowds flocking to the foretold place at the foretold time to witness it.

Now, nobody believes that the sun really did move out of its orbit and come crashing down to Earth. If the crowd believed that this is what would happen, they would have stayed at home and witnessed it from there; everyone across the day side of the world at that moment would have seen it. No: as prophesied by the young girl, Lucia, the vision would only be seen by those who assembled to see it, who had faith enough to believe what she said. This was a vision from God: not a physical occurrence, but a collective mental and spiritual experience, one that does not defy the laws of physics as we know them – nothing impossible occurred – but which nonetheless seems almost incredible, that so many people could have the same vision at once. That is why the Church proclaimed it to be a miracle, because it was so out-of-the-ordinary and improbable. Any one of the miracles recorded in the Bible could have happened in exactly the same way, with God using very improbable – but not impossible – means of surprising us into sitting up and listening. We can't know. God doesn't need us to know. He just wants us to know the 'good news' that in Jesus his promises are fulfilled; that he loves us, that he is always there with us, and that we can and should love him in return.

As if all this wasn't enough evidence to believe that the Gospels and the rest of the New Testament writings are a sound basis on which to place a good life – which is, after all, what all of us want ultimately to lead – and weren't just made up fantasies, the most important truth of these works is their sheer novelty and, frankly, their absurdity. Jesus' teachings – recorded by multiple people, as we have seen – could not be described as 'conventional', or as 'comfortable' for that matter. We are told that he condemned those traditionally exulted – the rich and powerful – while blessing the poor.

So far so good if you believe that the Gospels were invented by the poor to justify their own struggle for existence and improve their own lot in life. But Jesus also infuriated many of his own people – the Jews – by breaking their man-made laws and proclaiming new interpretations of God's law. He mixed not only with the poor but also with outcasts, enemies of his people, and foreigners – tax collectors, Samaritans, lepers – who were considered 'unclean' or even cursed by his contemporaries. He mixed with everyone, in fact, high and low, male and female, and showed them all the same deep love. Jesus had no respect for some of the things they did and said – especially the scribes and Pharisees – but he taught that we should love all our neighbours, friends and enemies alike.

Before his crucifixion, Jesus was rejected by everyone, utterly abandoned by all but a handful of women, whose testimony was at that time considered of little importance. He died the most shameful death, yet he rose again – not to a handful of witnesses, who could easily have made this up, but to hundreds or thousands. If you were to invent a story to create a cult following, aiming to inspire an uprising of the poor against the rich or the Jews against the Romans, this would not be it. You wouldn't set a crucified pacifist at the heart of a movement to overthrow the powerful. If you wanted to comfort the Jews, you wouldn't have their messiah as a poor carpenter who upset just about all their leaders, questioned all their assumptions and was ultimately betrayed by his own people. This was no fable invented by Matthew, Mark, John, Luke, Paul or anyone else. This was the Word of God, made flesh and dwelling among us: Jesus Christ, the Son of God. The New Testament is His testament.

3

Myths and Morality

The Bible's Old Testament contains a range of very different styles of writing. It was written over a long period of time, hundreds of years before the time of Jesus, by Israelites (Jews) and in Hebrew, their ancient language, rather than the Greek of the Gospels. And it doesn't claim to be a literal historical account of any particular life, nor friendly advice to worshippers. Indeed, few people believe or ever have believed that much of the Old Testament is literally true. It was never intended to be a literal portrayal of exactly what actually happened, and in recent times the only major movement that has interpreted it as such is that of the Evangelicals, beginning in the eighteenth century, who represent a minority of Christians. Those who wrote it down weren't scientists, like Luke the Gospel writer. Some of them were historians, but most of them were prophets who claimed to be revealing truths from God about the nature of God, mankind and the relationship between them. Such ideas were very important to the Israelites, whose belief in God stood in stark contrast to the religions of their neighbouring tribes in the Middle East, who worshipped multiple gods and idols. I've already explained the important difference between God and gods in Chapter 1.

Unless we're Biblical literalists – who in spite of vast scientific, historical and theological evidence to the contrary believe that all the Old Testament myths literally happened in the way they are described – we can place all the books of the Old Testament on a sliding scale between historical truth at one end and nearly entire allegory at the other. Yet all the books are equally useful when it comes to telling us about the human condition and the nature of God. They were mostly written down in the form we know them now in around 500 BC, when the Israelites were in exile from their own land (Judea, centred on Jerusalem), kept as captives of the Babylonian Empire which had conquered them and carted most of them off to Babylon. Looking back to reflect on how this had happened, the Israelites began to compile the stories that had been passed down by oral tradition and possibly in earlier writings for centuries.

The first five books of the Bible – the Pentateuch or Jewish Torah – Genesis, Exodus, Leviticus, Numbers and Deuteronomy, are all towards the mythical end of the scale. They were traditionally ascribed to Moses himself, the main human character of the story they tell, who led the Israelites out of a previous captivity in Egypt. However, they appear in fact to be an amalgam of many writers' work, and contain a few myths (the creation account, Noah's flood) that are common to multiple cultures around the world in different forms. The fact that they record Moses' death makes it very unlikely that he could be the sole author! Much more likely is that they were written down during the exile from oral tales and perhaps previous written versions that are now lost. In any case, they describe events thousands of years before the time of Moses, and cannot possibly have been literal blow-by-blow accounts unless directly recited to mankind by God himself.

At the other end of the scale we have the 'historical' books such as Chronicles and Kings. There is little reason to doubt (even for atheists) that much of what is recorded in these books is anything other than a true account of the history of the Kingdom of Israel, much like Bede's Ecclesiastical History of England or the histories of ancient Egypt, Rome, Babylon and Greece that we have. Like good historians, the authors of these books refer to their sources, which may have included near-contemporary accounts of what happened: often at the end of the description of a particular king's reign will come a sentence like, 'the rest of the acts of king X, are they not written in the book Y?'. These books make dramatic reading indeed, telling of the fortunes and misfortunes of the various rulers of Israel and Judah right up to the Babylonian exile itself. They are historical, but they are also moral: they relate how various kings were 'evil in the sight of the Lord' or 'did that which was right in the sight of the Lord' and were rewarded with good or bad fortune respectively.

The message is that if you don't trust in God and take his advice (given through the prophets), when things go wrong it's your own fault that you can't find a way out of trouble. When you do trust in God, bad things may happen but things come right again through his guidance. The God character in these stories is forgiving and merciful; when the King and people turn to him in humility and prayer, he restores their wealth and wellbeing time and again – this happens remarkably often. A human would have given up on the whole sinful lot of them when they'd turned to idolatry three, four, five times – but God keeps on forgiving. These books also tell us about the corrupting power of kings, and how they are tempted astray by their power (and their foreign polytheistic wives) and end up doing great harm to their people.

In the middle of these two extremes, mythological and historical, come various prophetic writings such as Isaiah, Jeremiah and Ezekiel, and proverbial books of wisdom such as Proverbs, Ecclesiastes and the Psalms. These books contain some of the most beautiful poetry ever composed, as you can understand best by reading a good translation – best of all, use the King James 'authorised' version for these texts, or the Book of Common Prayer for the Psalms, as its poetry is without parallel. The prophets lived during the time of the Kingdoms of Israel and Judah and the exile, and these books contain some of their words, purportedly passed on from God himself, and visions. They are the most difficult to read and understand of all the Old Testament, but they make it very clear – through extensive repetition across various contexts – what God our creator wants us to be, the deeds that he loves and those that he hates. Rich and powerful people abusing the poor, child sacrifice and rape he detests. Generosity, care for the needy, humility and equality – these are what he loves. Plus, we are told that he will send a King to deliver these things (a King that Christians interpret as being Jesus Christ).

Many Christians believe the prophets to be always looking ahead to Jesus, and it's easy to interpret their words as pointing to him (the Jews believe that the same scriptures point to a Messiah yet to come). The prophets talk of a future time when all the nations will know God – a key aspect of Christianity, which is followed by all sorts of people all around the world, is that the Jewish Covenant (or special agreement) with God has been extended to all people through Jesus – and they look forward to a new King in the line of the Biblical King David who will judge rightly and justly in God's name.

The psalms, too, often seem to be about the Jesus we see in the Gospels, although more often they seem simply to be reflections on the human condition and our relationship to God. They contain sorrow, elation, despair, pain, bereavement, contentment, thankfulness, estrangement from family, loneliness, praise, poverty, wealth, war, peace, anger, vengefulness and joy. Like the best poetry, a good psalm echoing the emotions one's feeling can be a great source of comfort. The psalms remind us that other humans have felt the same things as us before, even millennia ago in societies that were superficially very different from our own. Human nature hasn't really changed that much. Many psalms are traditionally ascribed to King David; he may well have written several, though not all, of the compendium.

Less likely to be true is that the 'Song of Solomon', another Old Testament work, was actually written by David's son King Solomon. This book, along with Ecclesiastes and Proverbs, is attributed to him because he is said to have been so wise, in a time when 'pseudopigraphy' (attributing a book to somebody who didn't write it) was less frowned upon than it might be today. The Song is a passionate poem of love between two people, which Christians have come to interpret as an allegory for the love between Christ and his Church – Christ himself refers to the 'bridegroom' and the 'bride' in several of his parables. Whether or not this allegory was the original purpose of the Song, it is a useful one because it reminds us that God's love for us is not passive and trite, distant and cold, but passionate and hot, like that between true lovers. God is with us and in us. Proverbs and Ecclesiastes, meanwhile, contain wise sayings and deep truths, like the famous 'Vanity of vanities, all is vanity' at the beginning of a passage which describes just how pointless many of the things we spend our lives doing actually are. How fleeting are the things we are so proud to build and create, the wealth we work so hard to earn!

What, then, is the purpose of the more allegorical books – the Pentateuch or Torah? Why not just have the wise proverbs and historical narratives? Jews hold the Torah to be the most sacred of texts, so much so that they parade the scrolls on which it is copied ceremoniously through the synagogue before they are read and try to touch them with their prayer scarves. Christians may, by contrast, read them from a battered old Bible, perhaps even annotated and scribbled in. They are neither the verbatim words of God nor even those of

Moses to most Christians (some Evangelicals excepted), but they are powerful reminders to everyone of the nature of God.

Let's start with the creation, the beginning of Genesis. Not many Christians believe that the world really was literally created in seven 'days' as we know them; after all, the Hebrew word usually translated as 'day' actually means a more general 'period of time' and, since God is timeless, what he means by 'day' could be billions of years to us! Elsewhere in scripture (actually in 2 Esdras, a book that doesn't appear in Protestant Bibles) a prophet speaks of a 'week of years', which demonstrates just how flexible scripture is when it comes to definitions of periods of time. Daniel's prophecy (in Chapter 9 of Daniel) about 'seventy weeks' actually refers to 'seventy sevens' in the Hebrew and is therefore often read to mean 'seventy times seven years'. If the word 'days' is interpreted in this way, the story of the world being created in seven 'days' becomes quite scientifically plausible, as we'll return to in Chapter 10. In any case, the most important thing that the creation story means for us is that God, the Father, created all things, and that humans were created – evolved, we might say – after other animals had long been in existence. It's a reminder to us to be humble: we are another part of God's creation, made last of all. We're not the most important part of creation – humanity is more like the jewel in the crown or the icing on the cake. That's the message of the early chapters of Genesis. It's intended to overawe us with the splendid story of creation, revealing to us our little place amidst this epic drama. A similar vision is given in the psalms: 'what is man', says Psalm 8, 'that you [God] are mindful of him?'

After the creation come Adam and Eve, the 'first people'. We might be better to say 'the first people to invent technology'. There were clearly other humans around – the Bible mentions how the 'children of God' mate with the 'children of men' – but they were the 'first' humans to evolve the mixed blessing of rationality. It's a story about the fall of mankind from that blissful (relatively speaking) time when we lived in simple ignorance like all the other animals, and settled down as farmers, working hard and tilling the ground. It's all there, in Genesis. First we were ashamed to be naked and invented clothes (the first technology), then we made tools for farming, then cities – and, yes, we invented murder along the way. We 'ate from the tree of the knowledge of good and evil' – we learned how to do good things and bad things, rather than just the things necessary for our survival. And we've been suffering as a result, ever since. We know today from science that these things must have happened at some point – after all, we're the only animals who wear clothes, till the ground and commit murder – but the story of Adam and Eve gave the people who read it that humbling revelation thousands of years ago. It's a story that tells us, among other things, that we've not always been the same – we changed (evolved) to be like we are now.

The early part of Genesis is a description of human evolution, and a lamentation over it! Noah's Ark is another myth designed as allegory, possibly based on some real event – the Black Sea appears to have flooded around 5500 BC because of a sudden inflow from the Mediterranean Sea, and some scholars have suggested that this may have given rise to myths about a 'great flood' that many ancient cultures in that region share. This story tells of partial redemption: when a human being (Noah) actually listened to God and showed love and compassion to other animals, he and his family were saved when everyone else, ignoring God's warnings, died off. Again, all of this can be related by Christians to Christ: he was the man who came to undo the harm that another man (Adam) had done, and the one who restored our relationship with God, for those who wish to interpret it in that way.

Exodus is another interesting book (compared to Leviticus, which isn't exactly a page-turner, filled with laws that instil in us a sense of being pure and perfect before God). It talks of the journey of the Israelites, having been captive as slaves in Egypt, back to the 'Promised Land' of Israel, led by Moses who was commanded by God to do this in spite of his protestations. This story is again towards the mythological end of the scale, but contains probably many grains of historical truth. Exactly what did or didn't happen 3000 years ago isn't important: the story is important to monotheists mostly because of what it tells us about our relationship with God, by whom the Israelites were delivered from danger. Indeed, the Exodus example is so important that it's referred back to time and again by Israelite prophets and is central to Jewish practices to this day.

The essential message of Exodus is that it's God who rescued Israel (the Jewish people), against the odds, God who chose them to be his people and cast out other (godless) nations to 'plant them in'. God carries out, in the story, wonders and marvels in Egypt to punish the Egyptians for enslaving his people, from swarms of locusts that devour all the food to hail so heavy it destroys the crops (but not the Israelites' crops) and cattle (but not the cattle of those who listened to Moses' warnings and shut their animals safely away). Pharaoh refuses again and again to let the people go because God 'hardens his heart' in order to punish him and Egypt, until eventually all the Egyptians' first-born sons are killed overnight by God's angel and the Israelites are allowed to go at last. Even then, Pharaoh changes his mind and pursues them, only for his army to be drowned when the sea parts for Israel but closes in over their pursuers.

It's an entertaining and somewhat harrowing drama, probably exaggerated and embellished far beyond historical fact, but it has an important point even for us today. The things that enslave us in this world, like the Egyptian oppressors in the story, will keep coming back again and again. Our only way to true freedom and salvation is to trust in God. Also, just as God hardens Pharaoh's heart, so it's God who makes the world like this – makes life a struggle when we swim against his tide or are tempted to do so – so that we can see all the more clearly the way he wants us to go. The ancient Israelites, believing in God, developed this myth and others like it to make this point. To what extent they were basing what they said on real events we cannot know, and it isn't important from the Christian perspective. The myths have been passed down to us as living stories rather than dry history, because the messages they contain about God are timeless. Stories like this are more enduring, more accessible and – importantly in the time before they were written down – more memorable than abstract statements. That's also why Jesus spoke in parables.

That's not to say the whole thing was necessarily made up. There is no archaeological evidence for an Exodus of hundreds of thousands of people from Egypt, which if it really happened should have occurred around three thousand years ago (the Bible isn't very specific with dates because it's not primarily about history), nor is it recorded in Egyptian records. On the other hand, nomadic people such as the Israelites wouldn't leave much archaeological evidence, and the Egyptians didn't tend to record losses and defeats, as they are said to have suffered at the hand of God when trying to stop the Israelites. What they did record was that Pharaoh Akhenaten changed the Egyptian religion to worship his Sun god alone and built a new city out of mud-brick in extremely quick time using slave labour – this could be why Exodus records the Israelites being forced to make mud bricks as fast as possible by the Egyptians. His successor Tutankhamun (around 1330 BC) was threatened with all sorts of plagues and disasters (including the sorts listed in Exodus) if he didn't restore the old Egyptian religion, and law and order began to break down, possibly because of such plagues. This was just the sort of opportunity the Israelite slaves would need to escape. Tutankhamun had no son to succeed him, so perhaps his firstborn did die, as the Bible story implies. It tells of all the Egyptians' firstborn – from prince to peasant – suddenly dying overnight, and suggests that this was the final painful impetus that at last led Pharaoh to let the Hebrew slaves go free. Thus, whilst there is no historical proof for the Exodus from Egypt, likewise there is a perfectly plausible point in the historical narrative at which it could well have happened.

Whatever the historical truth of the Israelites' flight from Egypt and their journey into the 'Promised Land' (modern-day Israel), the Ten Commandments that Moses is said to have given the Israelites from God during this journey must have come from somewhere, and there certainly were twelve Tribes of Israel, which the Bible explains by telling how Jacob (whose name was changed to Israel by God) had twelve sons who moved to Egypt a few generations before all this and whose descendants were enslaved.

People who believe the Genesis and Exodus stories to be, word for word, literally historically true are very rare (even many Creationists don't take it all as literal fact), and are concerning to many mainstream theists. Of course, these people are entitled to believe what they want to believe, based on their own assessment of the evidence they have, and it is not consistent with true Christianity, Judaism or Islam to advocate forcing anyone to 'believe' or 'disbelieve' anything (in fact you can't force someone to believe something, only to claim to believe it). Certainly Christ never forced anyone into belief, even when tempted to challenge the powers of the world embodied in Pontius Pilate. He didn't reveal himself in awesome splendour to be the Son of God; he said who he was, and let each person decide for his or herself whether they believed him or not.

However, Christ did tell Pilate that he came 'to testify to the Truth'. The sort of religion that pleases God is all about Truth. So when Christians see falsehoods such as Creationism emerging – which became prominent only around nineteenth seventeenth century onwards – we begin to worry that something other than Christianity is going on. God reveals to us the truth; lies and deception are blasphemy. They are an insult to God. It seems that many of those Christians who deny obvious scientific and historical facts are being led astray from the Truth revealed by God in Jesus Christ, quite possibly by unscrupulous persons who have other things than the will of God in mind. We must be very careful when dealing with people who refuse to change their picture of truth and falsehood in spite of evidence disproving what they claim, especially when they begin to teach things we know scientifically to be false to their children and are intolerant of any alternative explanations. These sorts of people are known as fundamentalists, and Creationists are one powerful example of Christian fundamentalism.

Is the same also true of Mormons? The Church of the Latter Day Saints, or Mormons, have what is essentially a Third Testament, in the form of the 'Book of Mormon' that they believe to be an Ancient Egyptian text translated by Joseph Smith into English at the direction of an angel in 1820s America. An entire Church was created around this translation, alongside the accompanying 'Book of Abraham'. Smith claimed to have translated these from papyrus scrolls discovered in Egypt, one of which was rediscovered in 1966 (the rest having been lost in a fire), but a modern translation of this scroll revealed a text entirely different to what Smith had claimed, adding weight to century-old suspicions that he had made the whole thing up. Yet millions of Mormons – mostly in America but now increasingly around the world – believe Smith's text to be valid, a genuine ancient text providing genuine truths about God. What are we to make of this?

Again, this question is important to Christians because Christians believe in truth. If Smith's translations are true, they should surely be adopted into the scriptural 'canon' – the official books used by the Church – as a third Testament. But if they are not true, either literally or allegorically, no Christian – including Mormon Christians – should treat them with any more importance than a work of contemporary fiction. The official teaching of the 'Catholic Church' (that's a term used to describe all the mainstream Churches including the Roman Catholics, Anglicans and Orthodox Christians) is that the Book of Mormon is not Holy Scripture, but the work of Joseph Smith. Most in the Catholic Church therefore don't include Mormons in that Church. But Mormons do count themselves as being part of the worldwide Catholic Church, and hold that the rest of the Church needs to catch up and adopt the additional scripture. It must fall, then, to each of us to survey the evidence and decide whether Joseph Smith genuinely uncovered important scriptures, or whether he and the early founders of the Mormon Church were frauds, perhaps more interested in their own power and wealth than in the truth, and act accordingly. The evidence for me falls upon the latter conclusion, which is why I am not a member of the Mormon Church.

Why, then, do so many Mormons draw the opposite conclusion, and why has God not revealed to them that their new scriptures are fake? Some would say, because he doesn't exist, and the whole Bible's a lot of nonsense anyway. I've already explained why I'm not in this camp. For the rest of us, then, who do believe in the Bible, there are two possibilities: either the Mormons aren't listening to God, and their Christianity is based on false teaching; or the Book of Mormon, even if it's not a genuine ancient text, is nonetheless an aid rather than a hindrance to their Christianity, used by God to inspire the Mormons to do his work. As we have seen, much of the Old Testament isn't literally, historically true, and wasn't written by Moses at all. Likewise, the Book of Mormon may not be historically, literally true (it claims that Native Americans descended from Israelites, for one thing) but may nonetheless be a useful fictional account that gives a true representation of the nature of God – another collection of parables. Where Smith dreamed it from – a divine vision, a dream, his own imagination – and what his exact motives were we cannot know, but this does not stop his words being allegorically true, or even inspired by the Holy Spirit.

So, then, let's look at the evidence. What does the Book of Mormon actually say? It purports to be the stories of Israelites living around the time of the Babylonian Exile in the 500s BC, about the time that much of the Old Testament was written. The Mormon Church, erroneously I think, holds it to be historical truth. Most independent scholars who have studied it suggest it is more likely to have been an amalgam of King James Bible stories with other Israelite texts that would have been available to Smith, along with a generous dose of imagination. Tellingly, it contains some of the translation errors present in the King James Bible but not in more recent Bible translations when it refers to Biblical characters and events. But what it says is not at odds with the Gospels – and indeed it has its main characters talking about Christ (hundreds of years before he arrived in person) – except for its advocacy of polygamy (which was common at the time of the Old Testament).

The title page of the book itself (one of the last parts of the text supposedly revealed to Smith) says that its purpose is primarily to encourage the revelation of the Gospel of Jesus Christ to all nations, and to illustrate that Gospel through its stories. In other words, it has a very similar purpose and place to that of the Old Testament in Christian eyes, and is of secondary importance to the New Testament (even if the Mormon Church hasn't always treated it as such). Once again, the proof of the pudding is in the eating: is the Mormon

Church demonstrably Christian, or not? The Mormons send missionaries across the world – indeed, this work is a requirement for all their members for a year or so on reaching maturity – who both learn from and teach to people of other cultures. This self-sacrificial act is more like what one would expect of a genuinely Christian organisation than one that exists for the benefit of its own wealth and power. What do these missionaries teach? Not primarily the Book of Mormon, but more often the Gospel of Christ, with its emphasis on love, faith and simple joy.

I don't believe that the Mormons are lapsed Christians, frauds or failures (though all human institutions have weaknesses, and a few individual members of any Church or any organisation for that matter could be any of these things). The texts of Smith, then, we should not assume to be evil; it is just possible that they are an inspiration used by God for good. Yet we must not take them to represent literal history when they describe the history of Abraham or the Israelite settlement of America. That would be to deceive ourselves.

The balance of evidence is in support of the conclusion that the Book of Mormon was written by a Christian with Christian ends in mind, but is not a genuine ancient text or divine revelation, and Joseph Smith was being fraudulent, and not very Christian, if he deceived others on this point. However, since 'those who are not against us are for us' according to Christ himself, a mainstream Christian need not be opposed to the Mormon Church, which is actively spreading the good news of Christianity around the world. Certainly, the Mormons' belief in the Book of Mormon, which directly contradicts historical and archaeological evidence, need not in and of itself be a cause to question a mainstream Christian's belief in the Bible as a source of moral, spiritual and – in some cases – historical truth. That's because, unlike the Mormon text, the parts of the Old Testament that are not obviously metaphorical do not contradict other evidence.

Anyone who thinks that the Old Testament is supposed primarily to be about literal historical truth is missing the point entirely. The purpose of the Old Testament is best summed up in the Book of Ecclesiasticus, which is contained in the Apocrypha (a set of books that are part of the Roman Catholic and Orthodox Bibles but aren't included in Protestant ones). This passage is in Chapter 2, where the author is describing what it means to be 'a servant of the Lord':

> Consider the past generations and see:
> Was anyone who trusted in the Lord disappointed?
> Was anyone who stood firm in the fear of him ever deserted?
> Did he ever neglect anyone who prayed to him?
> For the Lord is compassionate and merciful;
> He forgives sins and comes to the rescue in time of trouble.
> Woe to faint hearts and nervous hands
> And to the sinner that leads a double life:
> Woe to the feeble-hearted! They have no faith,
> And therefore shall go unprotected.
> Woe to you who have given up the struggle!

What will you do when the Lord's reckoning comes?
Those who fear the Lord try to do His will;
And all who love him steep themselves in the Law.
Those who fear the Lord are always prepared;
They humble themselves before him and say:
'We fill fall into the hands of the Lord, not into the
hands of men,
For His majesty is equalled by His mercy.'

The 'past generations' referred to in this passage are the people recorded in the Old Testament, and the whole thing is written as a set of fables – that is, stories with a moral. The main moral is that trusting in God, even in the face of fierce enemies (disaster, persecution, our own failings) is what will bring us prosperity – the 'Promised Land'. Turning away from God, as the Israelites do time and again with disastrous consequences, is to 'go unprotected' by him. The Bible's enduring popularity stems from the fact that, as well as telling us the Truth about God, it is also an intensely moral book, and tells us how to live a life that is genuinely good for everyone. It is filled with wisdom just waiting to be read and interpreted by those who are ready to ponder its verses and think for themselves, rather than lazily taking it as a mere historical narrative. The supreme goodness of the message such readers will draw from the Bible is the theme of the next chapter.

4

The Good Book

Who defines what is good? You might think the law, or our culture: some things are illegal because they are bad, like stabbing people; other things are culturally expected because they are good, like giving up your seat to a pregnant woman or a frail person on a train. But the law of the land is an invention of human beings just like you and me, and it rests of centuries of tradition – in other words, the law itself is derived from cultural expectations of 'good' and 'bad' behaviour. Sometimes, the human beings who shape the law get it wrong, and change the law so that good things become illegal or bad things are allowed. They might make it illegal for people of a particular minority group to own property, for instance, or legalise persecution and abuse.

That's the point when, in a free and democratic society, protesters start complaining and campaigning for a change in the law. They talk about human rights and animal welfare, freedom and oppression. When a democratic society (governed, at least in theory, by the people that comprise it) shifts its cultural perception of right and wrong, laws can change. Until 2018, abortion was illegal in Ireland. But many people thought that abortion was not bad, and shouldn't be banned after all, and started a campaign to legalise it. A referendum was held, the public voted in favour of legalisation, and abortion is now permitted in culturally acceptable circumstances. Hence, the law itself doesn't tell us what's good and bad: it only tells us what society regards as acceptable and unacceptable behaviour for an individual or corporation at a particular time. Society comes to a consensus, and the law reflects this.

Where does this consensus come from? In our society, it is mostly based on centuries of Christian morality: love for one another, and concern for one's neighbour. This morality has become so engrained in us that we have become quite different people to our less well-educated forebears. For the most part, people in our society today believe that violence, murder, rape, cruelty to children, abuse of pets, fraud, stealing and usury (charging people extortionate rates of interest) are wrong. This wasn't the case many hundreds of years ago. But since Christianity reached every corner of the British Isles in around the 700s AD, the central commandment of Christ to 'love one another' or 'love your neighbour as yourself' has been engrained in our public consciousness. It has informed our inner sense of justice, of right and wrong.

That's not to say that we always do what is right or condemn what it wrong, even if we have a nominally Christian society. There is always, in every one of us, an inner selfishness that says 'forget my neighbours: I'm in it for myself. I'm going to get rich, famous, powerful, comfortable – these things will make me happy. I'm not going to risk what I've got for the good of anyone else'. In medieval times, when everyone was purportedly 'Christian', some people were led by such selfish desires to deceive others into thinking they would be good candidates for Bishop or Pope, positions of leadership in the Church that began to accrue a lot of power and wealth, when they were really in it for themselves. These crooked bishops did a lot of damage to the Church and its subsequent reputation, peddling ideas such as the need to pay your way to forgiveness of sins (which of course made them yet richer). The Protestant Reformation was in large part an attempt to rid the Church of the greed and vice that had crept in amongst some (and by no means all) of its members.

In our own time, many people say openly that they're not Christian (which the medieval Church in a most unchristian way would punish you for doing). That doesn't mean they're not moral, or good, as we shall see in the next chapter. A lot of non-Christians are good people, but a lot are not, when seen through the prism of Christian morality. That's led to laws changing to allow some of our institutions to do very unchristian things – banks and loan sharks charging extortionate interest rates and evicting families that can't pay their mortgages, dodgy dealing and individual greed leading to financial chaos, corporations destroying the environment to make money. Many people who aren't Christian see this self-enrichment at the expense of others' suffering as wrong. That's because of our cultural inheritance of Christian morality.

By 'Christian morality' here, what I mean is the way of life led and preached by Jesus Christ. For Christians, Jesus Christ is God in human form. The doctrine of the Father and the Son as one God isn't supposed to confuse us: it's intended to make it clear that Christ is God, and God is Christ. The best way of knowing what our creator God is like, and how he wants us to act in His creation, is to look at Jesus Christ. 'I am the way, the truth and the life. No-one comes to the Father except through me.' That's how Christ himself puts it in the Gospel of John (chapter 14, verse 6). The Old Testament stories we met in Chapter 3 are all very well and good, each of them teaching us some moral or another, but they're not the best place to look for an idea of what God is really like.

God is a character in the Old Testament stories, often imbued with human characteristics like anger, jealousy and pity. He is there to play a role in the story being told. To see him as he really is, as he fully and truly is, Christians instead look to Christ. That's why, they believe, Christ came to us in the first place. And it's from Christ that we get a proper definition of good and bad. He teaches us about good and bad from God's perspective, an everlasting perspective, not the perspective of people who have written stories about previous interactions with God. If we believe that God made the whole universe and dwells in it and made us for his own pleasure, obviously what God calls good and bad are the very definitions of good and bad – we betray our own purpose in existence if we do bad, and fulfil that purpose when we do good.

God cannot be anything but good, because the whole universe exists for him and through him, so good is by definition what he wants! Yet God the Son (Christ) shows us that he is also present in all of us, knowing us intimately, and what he wants is therefore also what we want, in our heart of hearts, when all the distractions and difficulties of the world in which we live are put aside. God is love, goodness is love, and Christ demonstrates the greatest good that we can do, the very best thing in God's eyes: to 'love one another as I have loved you'.

How, then, did God look when he came in the form of Christ? Loving, merciful, forgiving, peaceful, self-sacrificing, giving, sometimes provocative, but delighting in others' joy. I cannot here relate all the deeds and words of Christ without copying out a whole Gospel, but I'll give you a few highlights to convey the flavour of his ministry. In the Gospels, Christ comes as a humble man, despite being the King of all of us and the maker of the universe in human form, and is baptised (dipped in cleansing water) by another humble man, John the Baptist. He doesn't show off or vaunt his power, just as God doesn't show off in our world today with Earth-shattering revelations or force us to do anything. Indeed, ask any Christian and they will tell you that they experience God as one who prompts, guides and whispers, rather than cajoling, directing, or shouting his will at us. Christ heals the sick, blind, deaf and lame, and pronounces that they can stop worrying about their previous 'sins' – anything they've done wrong – because they've been forgiven. He makes it clear that it's not as punishment for their sins that they were sick in the first place (as a lot of people thought at the time, which led them to have little pity for the sick).

Jesus isn't a stickler for strict rules for the sake of rules. He's not interested in pernickety religious points like not working at all on the Sabbath, because those in his day (or our own) who interpret God's law in this way are making the cardinal error of taking the Old Testament myths far too literally. He's not like the Pharisees – a strict religious 'party' in Jerusalem at the time – who insisted that everyone keep a set of hundreds of little rules that had been invented by generations of rabbis commenting on God's law laid down in the Torah rather than being commanded by God himself. They get very angry when he heals on the Sabbath. Christ says the Sabbath is a gift – a day off – not an obligation that should be borne grievously but an opportunity to embrace thankfully. The purpose of the Sabbath is to allow us to give one another a day away from our usual work, for the enjoyment of all, not to force each other not to lift a finger (even to heal the sick) on pain of death!

Jesus raises the dead, to show us that we needn't be too upset about anyone or anything dying or decaying or being destroyed in this life, because everything in Earth must end but we will all be resurrected to new life in the world to come. He comforts the mourning; he proclaims 'liberty to the captives' just as the prophet Isaiah foretold, telling us to stop worrying about all the things that imprison and possess us and get on with living lives of love. He teaches us to think for ourselves, reasoning with us through parables and comparisons, showing us how we ought to love everyone – even our supposed enemies – and to trust God as a loving father always ready to welcome us home whatever we might have done. He doesn't command these things out of the blue; he proves that it makes sense for us to think and behave like this.

Jesus allows himself to be arrested rather than put up a fight, trusting in God to carry out his will; he forgives his friends even when they run away and abandon him in his hour of need; he lets Pontius Pilate condemn him to death and suffers the most gruesome execution. Then he rises again to prove to us – with hard, fast evidence, in flesh and blood – that it's alright: God's will triumphs over a man's death; God's forgiveness triumphs over mankind's sin. That lifestyle is an example to us, both of how universally loving God is and of how we ought to be if we are to act as his children. Love one another, whatever the cost.

This was a profound and shocking idea to Jesus' contemporaries, as it is to many people today, and it seems that even his own disciples would have given up on it – and him – after the crucifixion, had Christ not been resurrected. All of them deserted him; his closest friend Peter flatly denied that he knew him. That Jesus' disciples are painted in a such a negative light is further evidence that the Gospel accounts weren't simply made up by them.

There's an important point concerning the crucifixion that needs to be addressed here. Some people think, when they read or hear about this story, that it must mean that God is a truly horrible character. We'll get to the absurdity of judging God's moral character later, but let's leave that aside for now. These people say, how can God be good, if he supposedly abandons his own son to die in agony on a cross, in order to forgive us our sins? If God is all-powerful, why didn't he just forgive our sins in the first place, without going through with all this horror?

Well, the answer is that he did. Nowhere in the Gospels or Paul's letters or conventional Christian teaching does it say that Christ had to die in agony on the cross in order for God to be forgiving. That's patently preposterous! God can forgive sins whenever he likes: a sin is an affront to God, after all, not necessarily to anyone else. He forgave people sins throughout the Old Testament, again and again allowing the Israelites a new start when they turned against him and followed false gods. He did it in the person of Christ, who was condemned by the Pharisee Jews long before the crucifixion for saying 'your sins are forgiven you' to people in the name of God. He goes on forgiving us our sins to this day. God didn't use the crucifixion as a mechanism for forgiving us our mistakes. He used this cruel, brutal act – which he didn't perpetrate himself; it was the Romans who did it after all, goaded on by the Jewish leaders acting under their own free will – to *show us* that our sins are forgiven. The difference is crucial. The fact that whatever wickedness we perform can be forgiven us was already known to God, but for us to know it for certain Christ had to die in front of us, by our own hands, and yet be raised again. The resurrection is even more fundamental to Christianity than the crucifixion – without it 'our faith is in vain' as Paul put it.

It was humans who committed this most cruel and gruesome act, humans who did the crucifying, murdering our own God. By contrast, it was God who did the resurrecting. And that's what God does throughout the Bible and throughout our human experience: making good out of bad. As humans, we get it wrong, we trash the Earth he made, we hurt and maim his children, we make a mess of everything – but God picks up the pieces, resurrects the dead, renews the face of the Earth (to paraphrase psalm 104). God is the God of creation and recreation, of healing and resurrection, of everlasting life. He is not the God of pain and death.

That's the picture of God we see most wonderfully in the New Testament, as Christians, and that's the God who inspires true Christian faith and morality. If you've ever experienced Church as dull, enforced, strict, loveless and cold, that's not Christianity. If you've ever experienced Christians as being sticklers for strict religious rules and regulations and 'thou shalt nots', that's not Christianity. Christianity isn't a religion; it's a movement, a following of Christ. Christianity is all about leading lives of joyful godliness, being God's children in the Earth: it's about shining rays of wonderful hope and light into a world blackened by the darkness of despair. God is all about faith, love and joy. We see it in Christ, and we feel it in ourselves. Anything that lacks any one of these things is not Christianity – or Judaism or Islam for that matter. If it's lacking in faith, love or joy, it's got nothing to do with God.

Brought up with a watered-down cultural inheritance of this New Testament vision of good and bad, some people have taken it upon themselves in recent times to look through the Old Testament doing a rather silly and pointless thing: trying to judge God on the basis of how he appears in those stories, and label him as 'good' or 'bad' according to the very moral lens that he himself showed us in Christ! They're using God's own moral compass to judge God's morality. I struggle to find words to describe just how ridiculous this is. It's like judging whether a flower is the correct colour by comparing it to a mere photograph of itself, or judging a politician by what their caricature says on the satirical show 'Dead Ringers'. In fact, that's quite a good analogy, because 'Dead Ringers' is an impressions show. The Old Testament is also an impressions show: the impressions that human beings have about aspects of God.

Whenever God appears in an Old Testament story, it's not God himself who's there, but an impersonation of God. Just as in an impressions show a certain aspect of a famous person might be taken up and magnified – a favourite expression, a nervous tick, or even a big nose – for comic effect, the Old Testament stories magnify individual aspects of God for dramatic effect. But they don't give us the fullness of God and what he's really like, just as Tony Blair's caricature on 'Dead Ringers' wasn't capable of running the country, and wasn't the real Prime Minister. It was only an imitation of one aspect of a man who would have had many more facets of his life that the public didn't see.

Moreover, just as in a political satire, some of the Old Testament is actually meant to be funny. Take the Book of Jonah, for example. It may not seem very rib-tickling to a modern audience, but this was cutting-edge comedy in the first millennium BC. Surely you don't think that at the time Jonah was written anyone actually believed that God had arranged for a real-life man to be swallowed by a whale, then spat up after three days? Or that this man would reluctantly agree to go and preach repentance to Nineveh, only for the whole city to put on sackcloth and pour ashes on their heads (a Biblical synonym for repentance) and be spared God's wrath to his annoyance? Or that God teased Jonah by giving him the shade of a tree that sprung up in the desert, then suddenly withered away just when he needed it? These are jokes, ancient Israel style. But behind the comedy lies a serious message, just as modern-day satire hides a serious message, often, and serious issues that people are struggling with.

In the case of Jonah, the moral is this: trust in God, do as he directs you through the signs he gives you, because if he wants you to do something – which you might be reluctant to do – he won't stop nagging you until you listen. There are other morals too. Jonah is very human and he gets angry at God because the people of Nineveh are forgiven, despite all their sins, when he'd been quite looking forward to seeing them get their comeuppance. But he learns that, just as he's upset when the fig tree he's sheltering under dies, God is very upset if a whole city ignores his warnings and gets destroyed. God forgives us because he loves us and cherishes us, and 'has no pleasure in the death of a sinner' as it is said numerous times in the Prophesy books. The idea behind the Book of Jonah is that we learn from what Jonah did, and what happened to him – because he's the human being in the story, so we can emulate him. It's not about learning who God really is – we only get snapshots of his true nature here – or trying to emulate God, because God isn't a human being in this story, so how can we emulate him?

Throughout the Old Testament myths, God is a character completely in control, who does what he likes; it's taken for granted that what he's doing is unquestionably right. The point of the stories is never to analyse the rightness or wrongness of what God does. We have to wait for Christ for God to come in human form, to get a picture of God that we really can emulate. The moral of Jonah isn't 'if someone isn't listening to you, throw them into a whale for three days and nights' or 'threaten a city with utter destruction if it won't do as you say', which is what the God character does. We're not being asked to play the part of God in our lives, but that of Jonah – and to play it better than he did. We get an idea of what God values in this story – forgiveness and mercy – but it was written by a human being, not by God, and for human beings to read. How can it possibly give us the full picture of God?

The same is true of all the Old Testament tales. Let's look at Adam and Eve again. Their fall from grace is what's behind the idea of 'original sin', nothing else than the notion that everyone makes mistakes, everyone acts and thinks selfishly sometimes, and this weakness is common to the whole of humanity – to all Adam's descendants in other words. That we all make mistakes is quite obviously true, whether or not you believe in

God, and you don't have to call it 'original sin' if that sounds too grandiose and judgemental – 'human nature' will do. Ever since we ceased to act like all the other animals (who are obedient to God because they act as nature directs) and evolved sufficient reason to do good and bad – the Bible uses the metaphor of eating from the 'tree of the knowledge of good and evil' – we have done bad things to one another and to God. We have suffered war, violence, disease, poverty, inequality and countless other things because of this evolution of rationality: it's like a double-edged sword, our greatest blessing and our greatest curse.

That's the whole point of the story of Adam and Eve. It's not that there really was an 'Adam', an original sinner. Adam is a character representing the earliest modern humans. Nor is God cruel to throw Adam and Eve out of the Garden of Eden: Eden represents blissful ignorance, and we left Eden when we evolved rationality and started inventing technology. Of course, God knew that this would happen – he is outside time and knows all time simultaneously – but he didn't stop it happening, in spite of all the suffering it would involve, because he wanted us to develop into something more than the rest of the animals, into rational agents able to choose to love him. The writer of that part of Genesis – who was quite possibly told this story in a vision from the Holy Spirit – makes up a character for God who oversees the whole thing, who doesn't cause the 'original sin' but sees it happening and pronounces the consequence.

Again, this is just a human projection of God, which in this particular case is designed to show us God's sorrow for our sin. It's not supposed to be an accurate depiction of what God actually 'felt' or 'said' thousands of years ago. God isn't really a human being, an 'old man in the sky'. He doesn't feel and say things like we do – except when he's in the form of Jesus Christ. The concept of original sin isn't a sign that God hates us and condemns even new-born babies as 'sinners'. It's just a statement of fact: that all of us are flawed, make mistakes and do bad things, to a greater or lesser degree. A baby has 'original sin' not because he or she has done anything bad – of course they haven't – but because when they grow up, they will do. It's inevitable. Within each human baby lies the potential for future flaws; that's what 'original sin' means. It doesn't mean they're going to be punished if they die before they leave the age of innocence!

Another story some people get upset about is that of Abraham and Isaac. In Genesis, we're told that God commands Abraham to offer up his firstborn son, Isaac, as a sacrifice. The two walk together into the wilderness, carrying firewood but no meat offering to burn for God on the fire: 'God himself will provide the offering', Abraham tells his son. They build the fire, and, though it pains him to do it, Abraham raises his knife to kill the child. At that moment, an angel from God stops him, and instead he sees a ram caught in the bushes to use. Isaac is saved. The problem that some people have with this story when they read it is that God appears cruel for making Isaac go through such an horrible ordeal, and Abraham seems to be a very bad parent for carrying it out. But the story, we must remember, isn't recalling the literal words that God 'spoke', or telling us what he actually did (let alone asking us to do the same).

Would God, seen most fully in Jesus Christ, ever tell someone to go and burn their son to death as an offering to him? Or put a child in peril of his or her life? Certainly not. The story isn't about what God does: to the ancient Israelites, God just does as he pleases, and there's no need to question his motives. This is simply a story designed to illustrate Abraham's faith, a faith so strong that he will give to God anything he has – even his precious son that he's waited so long to have – and devote himself entirely to God's service. Of course God doesn't want us to kill our children! Such is an abomination to God, later condemned explicitly by his prophets as the very worst of the Israelites' crimes. That's the whole point! Abraham has unbending faith, but he doesn't kill Isaac. Remember that Isaac was born to Abraham in his old age by a miracle, as a sign from God – God promised that Abraham's descendants would be so numerous they would fill the Earth. In that light, this story is about Abraham being willing to give back to God what God has given, to give up his only son, and yet still believe the promise in spite of everything. It's a gruesome way of telling us this moral, I agree, but that makes it all the more memorable, all the more powerful, at the same time as emphasising that we should never, ever sacrifice other human beings.

Nor is this story an indication that God loves animal sacrifices. At the time when it was first told and written down, people made sacrifices to gods. That's what they did. Hence the story's author used it as a convenient plot device. But God tells us in the prophets (which are less mythological, and a more direct picture of God's will, don't forget) that he hates animal sacrifices. 'Loyalty is my desire and not sacrifice,' he says, 'and the knowledge of God rather than burnt offerings.' The mythology uses animal sacrifice as a plot device, but when we hear God's actual words to Isaiah, Jeremiah and Ezekiel among others, he makes it very clear that it's not animal sacrifice that pleases him.

Why, then, is animal sacrifice seemingly commanded in the 'law' books, Leviticus and Deuteronomy, where there are quite specific instructions about which animals are to be sacrificed, how, when and by whom? Well, the purpose of these offerings is, the books tell us, that they are to be 'peace offerings', 'free will offerings' and an 'atonement', alongside other offerings of flour and oil. In other words, animal sacrifices are meant as atonement – an apology – to God for the sins of the Israelites, to sue for peace by freely giving him a gift. It's a practice that was borrowed from the pagan peoples worshiping other gods. But this time the sacrifice was to the one God, who created all things – including the animals the Israelites were sacrificing. It seems a bit pointless to sacrifice these animals to the God who owns them already, as the writer of psalm 50 has God say himself: 'if I were hungry, I would not tell you, for the whole world is mine and all that fills it. Do you think I eat the flesh of bulls, and drink the blood of goats? Offer to God a sacrifice of thanksgiving, and fulfil your vows to God most high!'

God's more interested in our giving him thanks and praise then, not the flesh of animals. But we have to remember that the Israelites kept animals, and would regularly kill some of them for meat. What they were doing, in offering the best and choicest of these to God, was giving back to him the best as an apology for taking for themselves the rest. Such sacrifices wouldn't be necessary if they weren't already taking God's animals and killing them; they're like an acknowledgement of the fact that what they are eating is actually God's.

The point of all this isn't, then, that God wants us to sacrifice animals: it's that we should give to him the best of what we have (why not, since he made us and our joy is his joy?) and acknowledge that everything that we have is given by him. By 'give him our best' I don't mean burning things on a bonfire to offer in sacrifice. That would be pointless. I mean using our talents, our skills, and our possessions to do God's work of loving one another. Indeed, the physical sacrifices the Israelites made were symbolic: like what's called a 'sacrament' in the modern Church (baptism for example) these sacrifices meant nothing unless they acted as an outward sign of an inward, spiritual truth. God isn't interested in the offering itself, which is just a symbol. He's interested in what it represents: the person who offers it repenting of their wrongdoing and giving their heart to God. Without that, the sacrifice is worthless to him.

Furthermore, the meat the Israelites offered wasn't supposed to be burnt to a crisp as if God had somehow 'eaten' it like a pagan anthropomorphic deity. It was to be roasted and eaten as food by God's servants – the members of the tribe of Levi, who unlike the other eleven tribes of Israel didn't have any land to work or animals of their own. They lived amongst the other tribes and worked as priests and Temple assistants; the meat offerings (flesh, flour and oil) were their food.

When we read the law books in the Old Testament, part of those first five 'books of Moses' that tell the stories of the early history of Israel, it's presented as though God commanded all these things in black and white – indeed on tables of stone – to Moses. This is a useful way of setting out the fact that the laws – those on animal sacrifice, those on forbidden and clean meats, those about observing the Sabbath day and all the rest – were what was necessary for the Israelites to live a godly live and to please God and themselves. But again, it's a story. We mustn't take what the storyteller says too literally. God didn't in reality – and still doesn't – strike anyone dead because they disobeyed some small point of his commandments. When this happens in the Pentateuch, it's a plot device that makes it clear that God doesn't like it when we disobey him and do wrong. The laws of the Israelites, just like our laws today, would probably have arisen organically and gradually, reflecting societal beliefs and customs – albeit in the context of a society that believed in God and listened to prophets that spoke his word.

Abraham and Moses, I believe, were real people who did receive prophecies from God. However, their stories were later embellished into those Old Testament myths that we know today. One of those myths sought to explain where the laws came from, by describing encounters between Moses and God, and to explain why Israel was a special people by describing their rescue from slavery, brought into the Promised Land. But really a lot of 'God's law' was simply the law of their ancient society, not a fixed and eternal law that God pronounced for all people at all times and places. God's universal law came, Christians believe, through Jesus; for Muslims, it came through the Qur'an. Both are expressions of God's Wisdom, God's Word, revealed directly to humanity.

What, then, about the Ten Commandments, the most famous laws of all? Are these the exacting demands of a jealous God, half of them being about unflinching obedience to him? Are they everlasting demands to be obeyed by all people for all time? Actually, they are neither exacting nor demands, and although the character of God declares himself to be 'jealous' when he prescribes them – by which he means that he is jealous when his people go after other gods – this is, again, just an impression of God in this particular circumstance in this particular story. It's not a reflection of the true, eternal nature of God, nor was it ever intended to be. It's simply a way of describing the fact that when we walk off after other, false gods, God feels upset – for our own sake, since these gods won't give us anything but superficial and short-lived pleasure.

Why is it that the God character in the Old Testament gets so irate about worshipping 'other gods'? Fundamentally, because he doesn't want us to be misled by falsehood and talking to deaf, blind and powerless statues when we could be doing good and enjoying a loving relationship with him. Just how ridiculous it is to serve false gods is illustrated very nicely in one of the Apocrypha books, the 'Letter of Jeremiah'. Here the author (who calls himself Jeremiah) points out at some length the irrationality of showing reverence to blocks of wood that have been coated with gold and silver to look like fancy gods. Though 'decked in purple', he points out, 'they cannot protect themselves against rust and moth'; though plated with gold 'they cannot shine unless someone rubs off the tarnish'. If the temple in which they sit is burnt down, these 'gods' go up in flames; if someone comes and steals them to melt them down they are powerless to stop the thief. They can't pass judgement, right wrongs or provide any help in times of war or disaster. Indeed, they're of no more use than a 'broken tool' or a 'block from the quarry' sitting in the corner of the temple: worthless rubbish. Yet people give sacrifices to these gods which the priests 'spend on themselves'. Overall, 'there is no evidence that they are gods', Jeremiah concludes, 'so have no fear of them'.

Many people were duped into worshipping fake gods – material things that they could see – instead of God whom they couldn't see directly. Instead of living God's way, loving one another and saying sorry when they did wrong, these people used to make sacrifices to the fake gods to 'appease' them. They would give money or goods or animals to the 'priests' of the false gods who tricked them into doing so. Sometimes they even sacrificed their own children. They thought that, this sacrifice having been offered, they had bought the gods' favour and could go and do as they pleased, ignoring the poor and needy, acting selfishly and perhaps committing atrocious sins.

It's not surprising that God feels upset about this sort of thing, in the same way as a husband or wife feels when their spouse, whom they love, suddenly goes off with someone else who doesn't love them, who will abuse and exploit them, and by whom they are tricked into doing hurtful things. God is 'jealous' for Israel in that he wants to jealously guard and protect Israel, and be their one true God. He's not jealous in the sense of a spoilt little boy who won't share his toys. Certainly, the story isn't intended to advocate jealousy as a virtue, or imply that God actually feels jealousy like a human. But just as for the ancient Israelites, so for us today, it tells us that God wants us to give our devotion to him, not to idols of any kind – be they money, celebrities, possessions or anything else he's created. He doesn't want us to be 'materialists' who only believe in physical objects – parts of his creation – that they can see, hear or touch and forget about the bigger picture, the God behind and within it all whom we can relate to and be with in spirit.

For Christians, the Ten Commandments really aren't anything like as central as they're sometimes supposed by those outside the faith to be. Look carefully at the Gospels, and you will see that Jesus never even mentions the Ten Commandments. In fact, they don't appear anywhere in the New Testament at all. That's because they're not really a very comprehensive set of imperatives – if we treat them as imperatives at all. If these genuinely were God's only demands on humanity, they'd leave a lot of bad things 'legal' in God's eyes. They don't forbid incest, rape, child slavery, animal abuse, usury, or a whole host of other nasty things that the Israelites could have done. Nor do they forbid speeding, electioneering, computer hacking (unless that counts as stealing) or poisoning the Great Barrier Reef. How could they? Cars, computers and democracy hadn't even been invented yet, and Australia wouldn't be discovered by anyone who'd heard of the Ten Commandments for well over two thousand years!

The point is that these 'laws' could never have been meant to apply to all people at all times. In fact, they're not really 'commandments' at all: the only commandment of God, as given in the Old Testament and explained by Jesus, is 'love your God with all your heart, mind and strength and love your neighbour as yourself'. That's it! It could be argued that the rest of the Bible is just an illustration of how to do this. The 'rest of the law and the prophets', as Jesus says, all hang on this. It's all God asks of us. Nothing more and nothing less.

Have you ever wondered why each of the Ten Commandments begins 'thou shalt'? It's not 'thou must' or 'thou ought'. That's because if you read carefully the passages in Exodus and Deuteronomy (the Ten Commandments are in both books) you'll see that they're not so much demands as descriptions of what a life centred on the love of God looks like. God says in the story, 'when you enter the Promised Land, this is what you will do, because you will love me and be good in my eyes'. It's not 'this is what you must do in order to be good': it's 'this is what you will do because you are good'. In other words, faith in God comes first; obeying these commandments follows naturally from it. The whole story of Israel travelling from Egypt to the Promised Land 'flowing with milk and honey' is a metaphor for this people finding God and travelling from sinfulness into virtue. When they turn back to sin, that's when they're exiled from their land again. The Ten Commandments are a description of what a virtuous Israel looks like. It's not that you can earn God's love by keeping them: it's the other way round. God loves you anyway; when you love him in return and put your faith in him, he gives you the strength to live a virtuous and good life. At least, that's the way most Jews and Christians see it: our good deeds are a response to God's love, not a means of earning it. So this is how we should read the passage:

1. I am the Lord your God who made you. Therefore, you won't want to put any other gods before me.

2. You won't make any graven images and bow down and serve them – what would be the point of that, since you know that I'm the only God? If you love me, I will show you much love and guidance and mercy. But if you follow these fake gods instead, how can I help you?

3. You won't take my name in vain, claiming falsely to speak on my behalf when you're actually out for your own gain; only sinful and dishonest people do that.

4. You'll keep my Sabbath day, once a week, as a day off – my gift to you, and your children, servants, animals and guests, so you won't expect them to work either. I'll bless you with enough of the fruits of your labours in the other days so that you'll be able to take a whole day off each and every week and not have to worry!

5. You'll honour your father and mother because you love them; then you'll live a long time on the land God has given you and have children who honour you too.

6. You won't kill anyone, because you love me and I made them and love them like I love you.

7. You won't commit adultery, because you'll be faithful to me, to your spouse and to your neighbours.

8. You won't steal, because you will see that everything is mine, and I will give you all you need anyway so there's no point in taking things from others.

9. You won't falsely accuse each other of things out of spite, because you know I hate injustice and deceit.

10. You won't enviously even desire your neighbour's wife or husband, house or possessions (let alone steal them) because I've blest you and them, and given you all you need, satisfying your desires, and you will love your neighbour just as you love me.

God gives these commandments as illustrations of what a good life looks like. He expects us to keep them because we love him and our neighbours, not out of heartless duty. The Sabbath commandment is particularly interesting. This is a gift much enjoyed by devout Jews to this day, but sadly lost in our society for the most-part. It doesn't mean 'don't lift a finger on the Sabbath on pain of death – go out of your way to avoid anything that could be construed as work'! It means, if you love God, then you can trust him that things won't go wrong if you take a day off a week – free from the distractions of work, free to live with God and your family and friends and share time with them. God doesn't want our lives just to be filled with work, with no time to enjoy his creation. He made us so that we could enjoy it with him!

'Honour your father and mother' is interesting too. Certainly, it means that you will care for your biological mum and dad, but it could also be a metaphor for honouring father God and looking after mother Earth – that might explain the appendage 'that your life may be long in the land your God has given you'. Look after the planet, and it will provide for us.

The 'commandments' are all good things, reassuring things. The writer of this story knew what he was talking about, and I'm sure the Ten Commandments did come from God, and that it's no bad thing if the Jews or Christians – or anyone else – of today live lives in accordance with them, a sign that they are in God's 'Promised Land' as individuals and as a faith community. But they are just an illustration, some useful examples of what it's like to be in this Promised Land, to live in faith. They are by no means the best statement of what God really desires of us: to love one another.

I hope that these examples from the Old Testament are sufficient for you to get the picture; I could go on with many more. The main point is that much of the Old Testament is myth, and most of the characters in it – including the God character – are just that, conceptions designed to convey a moral message rather than representations of real people. As I have said, I think, in all likelihood, that Abraham, Jacob, Moses and the rest were real people, but their sayings and actions were mythologised by their later descendants, who wrote impersonations of them to put across the right message. The Old Testament, after all, is full of wise sayings – it's designed to instil wisdom about the purpose of life and how to live; it's not meant to be an accurate biography of ancient Jews. Likewise, the God who appears in these myths is a character moulded to suit the story.

For the ancient Israelites, God was all-powerful, and any event not caused by humans must therefore have been caused by God – something that many theists still believe to be true today. So when they say things like 'God sent a plague' or have God say, 'I will punish you with famine', they're not really saying that God in all actuality sits there in heaven saying 'these people are disobedient so I'm going to strike them down.' No, rather God is in charge of all Earth's systems – including the weather and so on – and he knows when famine or disease is going to arise if people don't take the appropriate preventative measures in time. If we pay no attention to him, and don't ask for his help, it's little wonder that we fall victim to these things which we can't see coming but he can. If we still lived as innocent hunter-gatherers, we – like the other animals – would face few disasters: famine, rampant disease and warfare are caused by our modern settled, farming lifestyles. If we're going to rebel against him (as Adam and Eve did in the story) and live in this unnatural way, then, we're going to need to listen to God's guidance because trouble will come if we don't – not because of him but because of us! That's one of the key Old Testament messages: disaster is the fault of humans, not the fault of God, whether it's 'natural' disaster or manmade murder. We through our pride have set ourselves up for the fall.

Now, I know what many of those eager to 'judge' God are going to say to this. They'll say that all that I've written about the metaphorical and allegorical nature of the Old Testament is just what I've made up in order to 'apologise' for God and the Bible, to get Christianity and Judaism out of a tight corner and make them acceptable to a modern culture that is more sensitive than its ancient precursors. But the truth is that this is how the Bible was always read, for centuries. In Christian circles at least, the Old Testament has always been taken in the light of Christ's message and the nature of God revealed in him – as far as we know. Ideas about taking the Old Testament literally are very new indeed, and arose after the reformation as part of a newfound emphasis on scriptural (rather than Papal or kingly) authority amongst some Protestants – the Evangelicals especially.

There's nothing wrong with scriptural authority, as long as it's read with its context, purpose and limitations in mind, guided by God's spirit. But it's almost as if some (not all) Evangelical Protestants wanted to take every word of the Bible literally just to spite the Roman Catholic Church they were reacting against, which had traditionally placed the consensus of the Church and the Pope's word above the Bible in importance. At the same time, these post-Reformation Christians were eager to defend their world-view against what they saw as a threat from newfound scientific explanations of how the world was physically made. They were wrong to be afraid; science is no threat to faith – it is the deepening of our knowledge of God's world. To argue that the Bible 'contradicts' science is to misunderstand them both. To pretend that Biblical mythology is history and allegory is science is preposterous. As is the idea that, on the basis of a literal interpretation of these stories, God is anything but good!

The only sensible way of interpreting the Old Testament is the tried-and-tested way. The God character may be harsh sometimes, in deed or in word, or so it may seem to us when we read some of these stories in isolation. Those stories illustrate the fact that God sometimes chastises us when we do wrong, but looking at the whole picture given by the Bible we see that he does this as a father chastises the children he loves, not in the manner of a despot. It's because God loves us that he directs us. He guides us for our own good, and we do well to listen to him through whatever medium he speaks to us.

5

Good without God?

Now that we have seen how properly to read the Old Testament, and we know that God is good – in spite of the sometimes harsh things that he does in Biblical stories – there arises the question, is it necessary to believe in God in order for us, too, to be good? Obviously, nobody is suggesting that an atheist cannot do virtuous deeds to other people, or that theists are in any way perfect. Such a suggestion would be absurd. Loving one another is what, according to the Bible, God wants us to be doing, and atheists are just as capable of doing this as theists are. One cannot say that Jews, Christians and Muslims are always more 'good' in this sense than atheists are – indeed, many people calling themselves Jews, Christians and Muslims over the course of history have done some horrendous things to the misery of both God and mankind. So have atheists.

Some of the most grievous attacks in history have been perpetrated against people of faith. All sorts of dubious characters, from Martin Luther to Adolf Hitler, have claimed to be carrying out a kind of divine retribution in the name of Christianity against the Jewish people, for example. The Jews have been blamed by such characters for supposedly causing the death of Jesus, a wicked perversion that brushes aside the fact that Jesus himself and all his earliest followers were Jews, God sent him to save the Jewish people with whom he had always had a special relationship, and punishing people for the sins of their forebears is explicitly condemned in the Bible and is a hateful, not a loving, thing to do. Martin Luther may have been a Christian in some respects, but his attitude in this instance was far from Christian; Hitler was not really a Christian at all (he pretended to be all things to all people to garner support and was a chronic liar). Indeed, anyone can use the name of religion of whatever sort to try to justify their own bigoted beliefs, or to stir up hatred against a scapegoat. The question we need to ask is, do such people do bad things because of their faith in God, or do they use faith to excuse it? And, furthermore, can atheists get the same impetus to be good as theists? Do we need God to be good?

The first myth that we must dispense with in this chapter is the idea that belief in God or lack of belief in God is a cause of evil deeds in and of itself. For all the crimes committed by people claiming to be acting in God's name – the Crusades in which Christians attacked 'infidels', violent Jihads waged by Muslims, anti-Semitic mass killings, Reformation-era bloodbaths and bonfires, and so on – we only need to look at Stalin's Russia to see that just as horrific deeds can be done in the name of atheism. Stalin sought to sweep away any potential source of opposition to his power and banned the Orthodox Church and all other forms of theistic religious devotion as part of a purge that saw millions killed.

Since the dawn of humanity, people have done evil things. Some have abused God's name to justify their actions, others have not. That to do so is wicked in

God's eyes is what the commandment 'you shall not use God's name in vain' is all about: nobody truly godly does that. Most onlookers would agree that Islamist groups such as Al-Qaida and the Taliban who commit murder, rape, oppression and forced conversion and claim to be Islamic when they do so are liars. Just look at the majority of Muslims in the world and you will see that such wickedness is not what their religion is about. Of course, the Bible, the Qur'an and any other Holy Book can be misread and abused to justify one's own evil intent, as can almost anything.

Usually, such misreading results from taking passages of scripture out of context. For instance, a devout Jew could seize upon Deuteronomy 19 verse 21, 'and thine eye shall not pity; but life shall go for life, eye for eye, tooth for tooth, hand for hand, foot for foot' to justify taking vengeance against an enemy, or anyone else who had broken the laws set down by God. But look more closely, and you will see that the context of this passage is very specific. In it, God – as the writer portrays him – is talking about what to do if somebody doesn't live up to the Ninth Commandment and bears false witness against his neighbour. In other words, if you falsely accuse somebody of stealing, say, and demand that they be punished by paying you back what they've 'stolen', you should instead be made to pay them the same amount. Or if you demand that somebody be stoned to death (as was a common punishment in the region at the time, there being no means of imprisoning criminals securely or executing them in less savage ways) for a crime that you know they are innocent of, you should be stoned to death instead. This part of the Jewish law isn't actually about vengeance or retribution at all. It's about punishing somebody who willingly and knowingly tries to get someone else wrongfully punished, to discourage people from falsely accusing each other.

Misreading and misusing this passage to justify retribution outside the very specific context for which it was intended isn't anything new: indeed, it was happening in Jesus' own time. He addressed the issue specifically, as recorded in the Gospel of Matthew: 'ye hath heard that it has been said, an eye for an eye and a tooth for a tooth: but I say unto you, that ye resist not evil, but whosoever shall smite thee on the right cheek, turn to him the other also. And if any man will sue thee at the law and take away thy coat, let him have thy cloke also.' This is God speaking to us, trough Christ, about how he wants us to behave. It's an inspiration for doing good to one another, and not doing evil on the basis of misinterpreted metaphorical scriptures. Jesus goes on, 'love your enemies, bless them that curse you, do good to them that hate you... that you may be the children of your father which is in heaven, for he maketh the sun to rise on the evil and the good.' In other words, God loves everyone, and we should do the same. Judgement for the wicked will come after this world; it's not up to us to mete it out on our neighbours here and now. That's the message, and by any standards it is good.

Jesus had a very clear message for those who sought to use the law of the Israelites, already 1000 years old in his day, to inflict burdens and punishments on others. Many of these were Pharisees, who not only held to the core of the Jewish law as described in the Torah (none of which Jesus explicitly contradicted) but also to centuries' worth of additional little rules and regulations that had arisen from subsequent rabbis' interpretation of the Biblical law. Very often, these interpretations were very strict and difficult to keep, which made the Pharisees feel very self-important for being better able to keep them than the common people, who would struggle to remain 'pure' while getting on with the daily business of their lives. The Pharisees looked down on 'sinners' and reprimanded them for their failings.

For example, trying to trick him, some of the Jewish leaders brought before Jesus a woman who had been caught in the act of adultery. If the Old Testament law were to be taken seriously, they argued, she ought to be stoned to death. Their interpretation of the law was that she was wicked and impure, and must be purged from society, whilst they were upright and honest. Jesus' response, recorded in John's Gospel, painted a different picture. Instead of condemning the adulterous woman, Jesus confronted her accusers with their own sin: 'he that is without sin among you, let him first cast a stone at her.' One by one, we are told, all her accusers departed in shame. They may outwardly have kept their strict Pharisaic rules to the letter, but deep down they all knew that they, too, had sinned.

Jesus, giving voice to God, made it plain that we have no right at all to punish each other for being sinful, because we are all capable of doing wicked things. Rather, we should try to understand each other and why we have acted in a sinful way, to forgive one another, to recognise that we are all one in God and to love one another. If the law were to be carried out literally to the letter, as the Pharisees might interpret it, we would all have to be stoned. But if Christ's law – God's law – is carried out, we'll all be forgiven if we show remorse. Jesus made it very clear that this is how God wanted the Old Testament laws to be interpreted in the first place, in Matthew chapter 5: 'think not that I am come to destroy the law and the prophets: I came not come to destroy, but to fulfil'. In other words, Christ is the fulfilment of Old Testament prophecy, and at the same time reveals to us the correct interpretation of the Old Testament law.

Some people try to find instances of Christ acting in an apparently 'bad' way in the Gospels – despite the fact that our cultural concepts of 'good' and 'bad' are grounded in centuries of Christianity anyway – in order to argue that Christianity, or perhaps even God himself, is anything other than good. But true Christianity – following Christ – is manifestly good in God's eyes, and is for the good of all creatures in Earth, and one can see this goodness permeating through every one of Christ's deeds and words. He, alone amongst all human characters in the Bible, was faultless, as we can see if we look properly at what the Gospels tell us.

One passage those keen to criticise Christ take issue with is his treatment of a fig tree in Matthew chapter 21: 'and when he saw a fig tree in the way, he came to it, and found nothing thereon, but leaves only, and said unto it, "let no fruit grow on thee henceforward for ever." And presently the fig tree withered away.'

What's this? Is Jesus being vengeful, exacting punishment on a tree for not giving him fruit out of season? Poor fig tree! What a wicked thing to do! But it's obvious to me, and I'm sure it is to you too, that this story is not about vengeance at all. The fig tree is part of God's creation. It is not sentient, and has no agency or feelings of its own. Why would God be exacting vengeance on it? Rather, this is God using part of his creation – the fig tree – to provide a powerful illustration of the truth, like a parable but in physical form.

Jesus himself goes on to tell us why the fig tree was withered, to illustrate the power of prayer: 'verily I say to you, if ye have faith and doubt not, ye shall not only do this to the fig tree, but also if ye shall say into this mountain, be thou removed and cast into the sea, it shall be done. And all things whatsoever ye shall ask in prayer, believing, ye shall receive.' An incredible promise, illustrated by the incredible feat of causing a fig tree to die by word alone, but one that I know from my own experience of prayer to be true. The fig tree also serves another purpose: to show us that, if God comes to us and surveys our lives, looking for good fruit – which is often used in the Bible as a metaphor for the good that we can choose to do, fruit of love, joy and faith – and finds none, our lives are worthless and we might as well be dead, like a tree that bears no fruit. It's true, isn't it? If you live your life never being good or kind or thankful to anyone, never experiencing love or joy, what's left of you that's of any value? All the value in our lives derives from our love of one another and our relationships.

Another accusation made against Jesus is that he was just a man of his time, prejudiced in the same way as his contemporaries were. If this man was the Son of God, it is said, why didn't he set the record straight in some of their erroneous beliefs, and reveal the scientific truth to everyone? Why didn't he teach his followers about evolution, the Big Bang and the creation of the world over billions of years, instead of those Genesis stories? Why, instead of just healing demon-possessed men, didn't he reveal to them the truth that there are no actual physical 'demons', just mental and emotional conditions that mean some people have special need of help? Why didn't he reveal to the world all the wonders of modern science? The answer is quite simple: because modern science, wonderful as it is, isn't all that important. Not when compared to the truth that Jesus had really come to reveal, the truth of God's love.

Don't mistake my meaning here: I love science. I know that the wonders science has revealed about the universe are fascinating, and inspire a lot of joy, wonder and excitement. I know, indeed, that science reveals the splendour of God's creation and constitutes a form of worship of God. But part of our delight in scientific truths comes from our discovering them for ourselves. The sort of truth that God doesn't leave us to work out on our own, because it is so important to how we live our lives and how we feel every day, is moral truth. The fact that God loves us so much that he'd give his own life for ours (which, in creating us out of himself he has in a sense already done), the fact that we ought to love each other in the same way – these are the fundamental truths that Christ came to reveal. He didn't replace the Genesis myths with a more exact scientific account because of the same motivation that led to these myths being given us in the first place: all the important moral truths are contained in Genesis already, in the form of stories that people can easily remember and everyone can understand, whether they lived in Jesus' time or our own. Could the same be said of modern cosmology and quantum physics?

That we have now discovered more about how God physically created the world is interesting, but it's not really as important as the knowledge that God created us, and everything else. It wasn't because Jesus was 'just a man of his time' who didn't know better – though, as he was in human form, we cannot expect him to have had the whole knowledge of God contained in his human brain anyway. I'm quite sure he knew there wasn't an evil creature called a 'demon' that would physically enter into a person and make them mentally ill, as some of his contemporaries might have thought. But that didn't mean he couldn't use 'demon' as a metaphor in the same way as we do today, to describe the emotional and psychological 'demons' that really do haunt us within our own minds, and couldn't heal those 'possessed' of these problems through a metaphorical exorcism when he miraculously cured. The truth is that mental illness can feel like a 'demon' that possesses, or takes over, the victim. Why should Jesus refute the existence of something so palpably real in the minds of sufferers, on the basis of a narrow post-enlightenment definition of 'demon' invented centuries after their time?

God's truth, which Christians believe is revealed to us in Jesus, is an everlasting truth. It's not like scientific truth, of which we can never be one hundred per cent sure, such as 'nothing can travel faster than the speed of light'. That's a physical 'law', which scientists believe to be true on the basis of observations and experiments, but we might find out one day that it's not strictly true after all, it's just an approximation of some deeper law. Or we might not. We can't know for sure. All scientific 'truths' are subject to replacement by new, deeper understandings as science progresses. God's law, on the other hand, never changes – as Jesus himself tells us: 'love one another' is a law we can be certain of, in all times and places, because it's not something we had to figure out ourselves through experiments and isn't based on the evidence of our senses. It's something God has revealed to us – in scripture, in Jesus, and in our hearts – because it's fundamental to how we live and who we are.

What about the idea that Jesus was unkind to his mother? For some reason, some critical commentators take issue with his words to Mary at a wedding in Cana reported in John's Gospel. This was supposedly the scene of his first miracle, that of turning water into wine. Mary is told that the wine for the wedding feast has run out, and asks Jesus to do something about it. He replies, 'woman, what have I to do with thee? Mine hour has not yet come.' Now, some people get upset at Jesus' use of the world 'woman' here in a way that might imply that he – or, at least, the Jesus that John portrays him to be – is being degrading of women. But why take his words in

111

such an uncharacteristically demeaning tone? The word for 'woman' that John uses has connotations in the Hebrew of love and affection, and could be translated 'beloved woman'. The 'what have I to do with thee?' sounds to my ears like a playful, joking remark, something that is evidenced by the fact that Jesus performs the miracle anyway, conforming to his mother's request like any good son, rather than leaving her in the lurch because he doesn't think he's supposed to be performing public miracles yet!

The story in truth illustrates Jesus' great love for his mother, a love that he in fact has for everyone willing to receive it, as he makes clear when he announces 'behold my mother and my brethren!' to the whole crowd of people listening to him as recorded in chapter 3 of Mark's Gospel. Indeed, in chapter 7 of Mark we are told that Jesus criticised the Pharisees and Scribes for using religion as an excuse not to care for their parents properly. At the same time, though, Jesus was honest about the fact that serving God and loving others might sometimes cause friction with your family, friends and life prospects in the eyes of the world: 'if any man come to me, and hate not his father, and mother, and wife, and children, and brethren, and sisters, yea and his own life also, he cannot be my disciple' he says in Luke. But the word 'hate' here is not intended as an opposite to love, as in 'despise': Jesus clearly demonstrates his love for everybody. He follows this statement with a parable about having to count the cost before you start building something, making it clear that by 'hate' he means 'be willing to renounce' or even 'sacrifice enjoying'. In other words, to follow Christ the Christian may need to leave behind their family, or even be rejected by them: they must not allow themselves to be prevented from doing good by their family's expectations and demands. Doing what is good and right is more important than having a comfortable life or being popular.

Admittedly, this is not the easiest thing for somebody to hear. But Christ's religion isn't easy. I've already explained how, in the 'western' culture, so much of what he lived and taught has been engrained into our cultural understanding of 'right' and 'wrong'. But Christ's way cuts so much against the grain of our natural selfishness as human beings that his principles have only superficially been dyed into our culture in this way. It takes conscious effort, and faith in God, to be truly Christian, and to accept fully what has been called the 'selfless way of Christ'. If we read the Gospel fully and deeply, to love Christ is to love Him (God) more than anyone else, to put His law of love above fame, fortune or 'success'. God is what gives our lives their true meaning and purpose, not these temporary things.

To be Christian – or Muslim, or Jewish – is not just to pour in of our abundance money to help those in need, like a billionaire pouring millions into aid for the poor and leaving many more millions for himself, but to give everything we have to God's service. It is to become materially poor so that others might be made spiritually rich, to sacrifice the power that wealth and fame can bring, to love our 'enemies' to the extent that we offer more to the robber rather than trying to get back what he or she stole. It is to be humble, to take only what we need from the world and to give back even more, to trust ourselves into God's hands. That is what Christ shows us is truly 'good'. He trusted in God to the extent that he was publically shamed and crucified, and – Christians believe – was resurrected from the dead to show us the ultimate victory that this self-sacrifice precipitated.

That kind of 'good' is not common sense, it's not 'enlightened self-interest' (the idea that we do good to others only because we'll gain from it ourselves somehow) and it's certainly not simply sticking to a set of stone-cold commandments and rituals laid down in ancient books. It is a 'good' that springs purely and simply from genuine love of one another, good that reflects God's own desire and actions. One cannot be absurdly, self-destructively good like this without God. But only by being good in this way do our lives fulfil their true purpose and do we rise to a state of true joy.

So much for the theory, you may say, but to what extent are Christians, Jews, Muslims and other theists really godly? To what extent do they do good, as demonstrated by Jesus for example? After all, as we've seen already, people have committed all sorts of atrocities in the name of God. Aren't forty-two per cent of American convicted criminals Christian? Aren't Islamist terrorists Muslim? Weren't the majority of soldiers fighting in the two World Wars – and their commanders and rulers – Christian? Well, actually it depends what you mean by 'Christian' and 'Muslim'. For Christians, there's really only ever been one perfect Christian – Christ himself. Everyone else who's ever aspired to be Christian – to follow Christ – has fallen short of perfection in some way or another, since we all do bad things, just as no Muslim has ever entirely lived out the good life set down in the Qur'an.

What makes us 'Christian', 'Muslim', 'Jewish', 'Sikh', and so on, is our faith in God. We all put faith in God to heal us of our sinfulness; to make us more Christian, Jewish, Muslim, Sikh; to forgive us when we go wrong. No one can ever say, and I do not here try to argue, that people with this faith in God always do good and never do bad. Far from it! This world is so full of darkness and temptation that we all go astray sometimes. Nor do I say that people with faith always do more good to others than people without it do. But what I can say, with complete conviction based on my own and others' experience, is that faith in God leads us to do all sorts of good things – big and small – that we wouldn't otherwise do. Think of the Red Crescent, Red Cross, Christian Aid, the Salvation Army, and countless Mosque, Synagogue, Gurdwara and Church groups that exist to facilitate doing good and helping the needy in our communities, bringing together people of faith – and some people without it – to do good. The fact is that when a person has faith in God, though not perfect, that person will do more good and be more good than that same person would do or would be without faith. Let's not try to compare apples with oranges here: the murderer with faith against the charity-worker with none. Leaving all other variables constant – to make it a fair test – we find that faith improves the life of the person who has it, and makes them a better person than they personally would otherwise be.

6

God's Morality

To someone who has no faith in God, what I've written over the last few chapters may seem at times inconsistent when it comes to 'goodness' and scripture. How can a theist believe that some parts of Holy Scripture are literally true and historically accurate (God made the world, Jesus walked on water and so on) while others are just metaphors? In spite of the arguments I've given regarding the evidence in favour of much of the Bible's Old Testament, the Jewish Torah and the stories about creation and early humanity in the Qur'an being allegories whilst the miracles of Jesus were literally true, some atheists like to believe that theists just pick and choose which parts of scripture to believe in and which to downplay or reject.

Nothing could be further from the truth. As a Christian, I believe every word of the Bible, because it was written under the influence of the Holy Spirit. Muslims believe every word of the Qur'an. It's all true; none of it is rejected by believers as false – as Jesus said, 'it is easier for heaven and Earth to pass, than one tittle of the law to fail' (Luke 16, verse 17). When I read the Bible, I don't think, 'is this true or false, literal or metaphorical?', based on my own preconceptions about what God ought to do or say. My primary source of truth, remember, is not scripture – one can have faith in

God without knowing any scripture at all, if he is revealed to you by someone or something else in your life. The source of our faith is God himself. Scripture is an added enrichment, strengthening our faith and allowing it to be applied to human life more easily. When I read it, I do so prayerfully, asking God to reveal to me the truth in what it says and how to interpret that truth in my own place and time. Sometimes, if it's at a church service that I'm hearing the scriptures read, there may be someone there to preach a sermon that helps me to do this, to understand what God is saying to us today through these ancient but timeless words.

Thus, I believe in the moral truth of all the Old Testament, and I believe that all the miracles Jesus did really happened: they occurred as a physical demonstration of the truths that he taught. Jesus was not inconsistent. A prayerful, spiritual reading of (or listening to) what he did and says in the Bible reveals the true, loving nature of God through him. It is in the light of that love (which comes primarily through Jesus for Christians, but is manifested in other ways for people of other faiths) that the theist then reads the rest of scripture.

I'm saying all this to emphasise the point that God is the true source of the goodness that theists encounter through their faith. Our guide to good and bad doesn't have some other, secular source that we dress up as divine inspiration. It comes from God and it's illustrated in Holy Scripture. And it's this morality that has shaped much of our sense of 'good' and 'bad' in the world today. God has revealed moral truth in Jesus

117

Christ to Christians, and in the Holy Qur'an to Muslims, just as he revealed it to the ancient Israelites – the Jews – who were inspired to write their origin stories and devise a system of laws on the basis of it. These laws were revolutionary in their 'goodness' at the time, encouraging care for one another instead of selfishness, even if they seem sometimes outdated in our eyes, which have been enlightened by further revelations of God's goodness and purpose since they were written.

However, as I tried to make clear in the previous chapter, mankind hasn't always been very good at staying true to this morality, sent by God in so many different forms to show us how to live well. We become too easily full of our own self-importance, and end up refusing to listen to what God teaches us and trying to make up our own rules instead. Over the centuries, this self-importance has led some who claim to be doing God's will to be instead living by a philosophy known as 'absolutism'. Absolutists argue that there is a strict, black-and-white set of rules regarding what is right and what is wrong. They're the sort of people who look at the 'commandments' in Holy Scripture – such as the Ten Commandments – rub their hands in glee and say 'right, this is what we must and must not do – let's apply these rules rigidly, according to our own interpretation of what they mean (which we've made up to suit our own interests) and punish everyone who doesn't comply. That way we can look good and powerful and better than everyone else'.

There were lots of people like this is Jesus' time. They're described by the King James Bible as 'scribes and Pharisees'. And they crucified Jesus – for Christians, they crucified God in human form! That's because Jesus wanted nothing to do with their petty laws. One of the things they said was, for example, that because it says in the Old Testament 'thou shalt keep the Sabbath day holy', nobody should be allowed to do anything on the Sabbath – not even help someone else in need. What a perversion of God's will that we all love one another! They were furious when Jesus started performing miracles on a Saturday (the Jewish Sabbath), as you can imagine. They were also furious when his disciples didn't go through a washing ritual before eating, or when Jesus dared to suggest that a Jewish priest ought to stop and help a dying man he passed on the street – after all, wasn't there a law against a priest being 'defiled' by touching others' blood, or the dead?

Why were the absolutist scribes and Pharisees so angry? Not because Jesus was breaking God's law – he wasn't – but because he was threatening their own power over others, kept in place by their own over-embellished extensions to the law. In fact, that's exactly why they ended up having Jesus crucified – they killed God for daring to break the very absolutist laws that he had supposedly (according to their interpretation) commanded them to keep! It's no wonder Jesus accused them of being hypocrites.

As you can probably tell, I don't believe that God is an absolutist. I wouldn't blame you if you'd got the impression that he was, because some very self-important people in recent times have tried their best to persuade the world that he is. Years ago, the authorities of the land made it compulsory to go to Church, not because God wanted people to be forced into the pews but so that everyone could be kept in check by the secular powers. In our own day, the Roman Catholic Church has made clear its own view – which it is quite entitled to hold – that no foetus should ever be aborted, no matter how early in a pregnancy, because to Roman Catholics this somehow constitutes murder, a view that many people would disagree with. The problem is that the Church has laid down this interpretation as if it were an edict from God, a hard-and-fast rule that must be obeyed on pain of hell fire and damnation. It's done the same for contraception, for the ordination of women priests, and even for homosexuality – all banned outright as if they are irredeemably and without exception wrong in God's eyes.

Now, I only have to glance at the Gospels to know that that's not how God's morality works. Jesus' one commandment, as we saw before in Chapter 4, was 'love one another'. Christianity – real Christianity – has never been about hard-and-fast rules, except this one. Neither have any of the other followings that have God at their centre. It's all about gathering the evidence, considering the consequences of your actions, and acting on the basis of what in your heart you feel to be the most loving and joy-giving course of action. That's because God isn't interested in 'religion' as such at all. Christianity – at least, true Christianity in the sense of 'following Christ' as opposed to doing whatever the established church tells you – isn't a religion. Religion is about strict laws and principles; the Scribes, Pharisees and medieval Church hierarchy were very religious. Christianity isn't about laws; it's about love.

Do you think that God was looking on in glee when the Catholic and Protestant rulers started burning one another's followers on the stake at the Reformation for breaking one another's rules? Do you think that Jesus would have approved of such actions? Do you think that the people who perpetrated such atrocities really thought that he would? Of course they didn't – not really. What they were really interested in was securing their own position, their own power. Henry VIII, 'bloody' Mary and many of the sixteenth-century Popes weren't interested in what God actually wanted, but what they themselves selfishly desired. We all, as human beings, are just as guilty as them of acting selfishly ourselves sometimes. Jesus, on the other hand, gave up his own life rather than oppose those who made him their enemy. Those absolutist rulers murdered people on mass, and you can't get less Christian than that.

Interestingly, this atrocity was foreseen by one of the Old Testament stories that best illustrates the conflict between human and divine authority. The Book of Daniel tells the tale of Daniel and his friends, faithful believers in God, who were carried off to Babylon in the Jewish Exile (about 500 BC) and made to serve the interests of the Babylonian King Nebuchadnezzar. Out of interest, it is especially noteworthy that Daniel is referred to as a 'man of science' in the text, and we know he was praised and promoted for his wisdom by the king.

One day, Nebuchadnezzar got it into his head that he would make a great big gold statue of his own head – he was quite a big-headed man – and enact a law that everyone must bow down and worship it as a god. As faithful monotheists, Daniel's friends refused, so the king had them thrown into a 'burning fiery furnace' that was apparently so hot that the men who threw them in were burnt to a crisp. It sounds a bit like the Reformation, doesn't it? Daniel's friends miraculously survived, and the incident turned Nebuchadnezzar's heart towards God; the real martyrs burnt on the stake in the 1500s didn't. But in both cases, the rulers responsible were interested only in getting everyone to bow down to them and the false images of God that they had invented to serve their own selves, not in truly serving God and worshipping him for who he really is.

The moral of much of the Bible is that a true believer in God should not be a moral absolutist: what is right and wrong is not chiselled in stone like the Ten Commandments (which, as we have seen, are more accurately seen as illustrations of what a good life should look like), but varies depending on the circumstances at hand. Fixed, rigid laws have a place in every human society: they are there to protect us from what we fear or revile or what might harm us. Even these 'fixed' laws may evolve over time as our collective conception of right and wrong changes through campaigning for change, the spread of information and the leadership of powerful people. But the moral code that each of us follows as an individual must always be adaptable if we are to be good in God's eyes, based on love rather than law.

Usually, the laws of the land these days are good and don't conflict with what is most loving for us to do. Sometimes, though, they aren't and we may be compelled by our conscience to break the law – like civil rights protesters in 1950s America refusing to obey racist segregation laws. What's morally right for you and I at this particular moment in time can't be prescribed by the government or the Church or any religious body of today, nor even by Holy Scripture – though this may guide and inspire us. Nor can we be left just to decide what's good and bad for ourselves – 'anything goes'. True morality has to come from God himself.

The natural consequence of all this is that someone who believes in God and wishes to live a good life in His sight out of love for God, should not be bound by the conventions of his or her own day. For this reason, the New Testament is sometimes criticised for endorsing slavery, because Paul writes in his letter to the Ephesians, 'slaves, obey your Earthly masters with respect and fear, and with singleness of your heart, as unto Christ'. He writes to his friend Timothy, 'let as many servants as are under the yoke count their own masters worthy of all honour'. But when read impartially, neither of these statements says that slavery is a good thing at all! On the contrary, Paul is quite clearly telling slaves to love their masters in spite of being enslaved, in the same way that Jesus taught us to 'pray for those who persecute you'. Slavery is very bad, but the way to abolish this badness and in the process create a lot of goodness is not to be filled with hatred for its perpetrators. Hatred is conquered only by love.

One can – and should – work for the abolition of slavery of all kinds, without hating your own slave-master. Indeed anyone who serves God must oppose all slavery, since we need obey Him alone as master: God alone is King, and to enslave someone is to assume a false authority. Hatred gets you nowhere, but love can transform hearts. Loving your own master is more likely to win you and other slaves freedom than hating them, something that Mahatma Ghandi displayed famously in the early twentieth century when campaigning peacefully for the freedom of India. It's like the Old Testament story of Joseph, who is enslaved in Egypt but rises to prominence by doing good to the Egyptian Pharaoh and interpreting his dreams for him. Joseph ends up not only freed but promoted to be second-in-command of the whole kingdom. The Church is lax and unchristian if it ever condones or fails to condemn slavery utterly, since God abhors it, in all circumstances in which it is a cause of pain and sorrow. But to condemn slavery and to hate slave-owners are different things entirely.

Again, the Church is sometimes accused of denigrating women, mostly because of Paul's words in his letter to Timothy, 'let the women learn in silence with all subjection. But I suffer not a woman to teach, nor to usurp authority over the man, but to be in silence. For Adam was first formed, then Eve, and Adam was not deceived, but the woman being deceived was in the transgression.' Now, if Christianity was an absolutist religion, this would be a law to be applied to all women, and would be the source of much suffering and inequality. But it is not.

These words that Paul wrote about what he 'suffers' (permits) at a particular place and time where women were treated as inferior teachers to men and were generally much less well-educated than men, are not an everlasting law. I don't for a minute believe that Paul intended that they should be, or that he would have any objection to ordaining women to the same positions of authority as men in the Church today. Jesus kept women as close friends, just as much as men, and I am quite certain that Paul – a mere human, like you and I and the other writers of the Bible – was not inspired by God in implying that because Eve was formed after Adam in Genesis all women are necessarily inferior to men! I suspect that he was using this reference to the creation story to justify an existing prejudice, which in turn he wanted to use to stop women gossiping or wearing 'immodest apparel' in Timothy's church – in short, to prevent them from 'tempting' and distracting men in the same way that Adam was tempted and distracted by Eve.

Since the beginning, men have been led into immorality not by women but by their lustful desires for women – and often the woman is the victim of these desires. Paul didn't want women in the churches he'd planted to be flaunted before the men, because he thought the men would be distracted and tempted to sin. This hardly seems, to us, to be fair on the women, but Paul was writing at a time when women's needs weren't really thought about and no woman was ordinarily allowed to take up any position of authority outside the home. Remember that Paul had no idea that his letters would still be in use like this 2000 years after he'd written them. Through the lens of 'love one another', treating a woman as inferior or unfit to be a priest solely because of her gender isn't excusable in any circumstance I can conceive, but in Paul's day many women wouldn't be sufficiently educated to be respected as church leaders – a woeful fact, but nonetheless the truth. Paul's words on this subject say more about Paul's society than about him, or about God.

Where the Church – which is a human institution – has failed over the centuries is in not championing enough the causes of slaves, women, non-human animals and other oppressed groups: these are exactly the sorts of persons that Isaiah tells us the Messiah – Jesus – has come to save. Guided by God, not by petty man-made laws such as those Christ criticised in the Scribes and Pharisees but which the church itself slipped into in later centuries, a truly Christian Church should be ahead of the game when it comes to equality and acceptance, and to universal love. It should have been challenging the societal injustice that for so long put women inferior to men by ordaining women priests in 994, let alone 1994 – which is when the Church of England finally got round to it. It should have been warning about our growing disconnection from nature and lack of respect for fellow beings when the Industrial Revolution began, rather than waiting for climate change to become a terrifying reality and using this as a spur for action. It should never have mislabelled homosexuality 'sodomy' when in truth the Biblical city of Sodom was destroyed – in the Genesis story – for evil sins like rape, and not because of loving relationships between people of the same gender, which scripture does not condemn. Indeed, the Church should outspokenly champion acceptance of homosexuality and bisexuality, which are common in the animal kingdom of which humans are a part, as being a natural part of how God made us. Such diversity is to be celebrated as much as the diversity of personality, appearance, temperament and everything else that makes us who we are.

The Church and other religious institutions have failed to do this not because of God but because of people. We are the ones who have failed to live up to his morality. How, then, can we hope to devise a moral code of our own? If we want to be good, harmonious and happy as a species, we must not look to human laws, prejudices and conventions. We must look to the one God who made us all and knows us all intimately, and ask him to guide us in doing right. Make no mistake: God's law is not a burden – he even criticises the Israelites' false prophets for talking about 'the burden of the Lord' in the prophecy of Ezekiel. God's law is a joy, a release: it is given to us for our own benefit, alongside all its Old Testament illustrations. That's why God hates us worshiping idols, false gods: they stop us from listening to him, to our own detriment. Following God's law – whatever label your faith assumes – gives life meaning and joy. What greater good could there be than that?

Part Two

Understanding the Universe

7

The Miracle of Creation

One day, you, me, and everyone else who has ever existed, woke up and found ourselves somewhere in the midst of an incredible universe. It wasn't the same day – at least, not in an objective sense. The year, the date, the hour, the second, was different for each one of us. Yet for all of us it was the same moment in our lives – Day One, the awakening of our consciousness. The sensation of being alive.

So what is this existence into which we have awoken? It is, most fundamentally, the experience of space and time. Nowadays we refer to three 'dimensions' of space, or axes along which we can move: forwards and backwards, up and down, left and right; but we don't have a conscious realisation of this until we are taught. We simply experience space, as a continuum, and move through it. The fourth dimension, time, is very different. It is, like the other dimensions, an axis along which we can travel, from birth to death, but there's no 'backwards' in time. We can preserve memories of things that have happened before, using photographs and stories that we tell, and objects from the past might be kept for a while. But we can never actually go back.

If I walk a mile to the left and then a mile to the right, I end up back where I started in space, but will have moved half an hour onwards in time, and there's no direction in which I can travel – there is nothing that I can do – to get that half an hour back again, or to restore the universe to the state it was in when I started my journey. We all know this, and humans have always known it. It is not something that has to be taught, and other animals too may, albeit with less comprehension, instinctively understand the dimensions of space and even that of time.

Humanity has existed for tens of thousands of years, but it is difficult to exaggerate the sheer transformation of our understanding of our universe – the contents of space and time – that has taken place in just the last few centuries. Think about your grandparents, then imagine their grandparents (or perhaps their great-grandparents if you were born this side of the millennium) as children. It's only a handful of generations – a blink of the eye in biology – but the people you are now picturing would have had an almost entirely different understanding of the universe to that we have today. In all probability, they would never have seen motorcars, electric lights or radiators. They would never have heard of quantum physics or the 'big bang' or 'Natural Selection' or any of the other modern-day theories that we are about to encounter in this book. It's quite possible that your great-great-grandparents – just six generations from you and I – couldn't write, and wouldn't be able to read what I'm writing now. Most people in those days – and for centuries before them – spent almost their entire lives within about 25 miles of home. That was their 'space'. They would know about events in history only as events in fireside tales; they could understand the deep history of the world only through what they had heard read in Holy Scripture. That was their 'time'.

Only in the industrialised cities were things beginning to change. For most people, up until the mid-nineteenth century, things were largely as they always had been, for countless generations before them. I'm reminding you of this, because it's very important to remember it when we think about the ideas which follow in this chapter. This chapter is about the wonders of the universe as we understand it now, as human beings. But our understanding is as yet far from complete, and our great-great grandchildren may know a lot more. The more we learn about the universe beyond our day-to-day experience, the more we reach out from the comfortable familiarity of our immediate surroundings, the more amazingly breath-taking its complexity becomes. In this and the following two chapters, we'll explore some of what we know about our universe, and in Chapter 10 we'll think about what that has to do with God.

Let's start with the really big – the vastness of the universe, if we were to 'zoom out' almost to infinity – and work our way down to the really small. Interestingly, the world around us of everyday life that we know and love (or not) lies almost exactly in the middle of our maximum zoom-out and maximum zoom-in. That probably says less about our special 'place' in the middle than it does about the limitations of our technologies and scientific capabilities: zooming out a trillion times is roughly as difficult as zooming in a trillion times! The truth is, that we don't actually know how big our universe is. It could be infinitely big, or one among many other universes in a 'multiverse' that is infinitely big. Or it might be not much bigger than the 'visible universe' that we can observe.

There are actually many different kinds of multiverse that crop up in scientific theories, but we don't have any hard evidence either in favour of or against their existence, so I won't spend too much time on them here. Our universe might be one among many, or it might be unique. We don't know, there's no conceivable way at the moment that we can know, and frankly it doesn't make the slightest bit of difference to us here. A 'universe' is by definition a package of space and time that is entirely separate from and cannot be influenced by other 'universes' – if other realms of space and time could influence it, they would be part of our universe too. In the multiverse scenario I mentioned just now, you can quite easily picture our universe alongside many others, arranged in some sort of (probably not very neat) configuration like snooker balls on a snooker table – all separate but on the same 'plane' as one another in a higher dimension. There is in that case what we might call a 'series' of universes, because things in series are distinct and may be very varied, but can all be lined up neatly in a row and considered one at a time.

The opposite of 'series' is 'parallel', and the other sort of multiverse that has been thought up is one containing many parallel universes. The distinction with parallel universes is that they all resemble one another to some extent, because they all begin as the same universe which splits into two, then into four, and so on up to infinitely many universes all with a common origin. According to this idea, at each infinitesimal moment of time, all of the already-existing universes split into multiple parallel copies of each other which differ according to the configuration of quantum particles they contain (we'll get to those in Chapter 9) whose behaviour cannot be predicted. That would mean that whenever you or I or any quantum particle makes a decision – left or right? speed up or slow down? wear red or blue socks today? – a new suite of universes is created with a different outcome in each one. It's a confusing concept much more difficult to picture than the series multiverse, and I don't blame you if you can't get your head around it – neither can I! To be honest, I find the idea of an infinite infinity of universes both difficult to imagine and patently absurd, given that there's not a shred of evidence for it, but I can't prove that it isn't true and we'll leave the whole question aside for now, and focus on our universe.

What we know about our universe comes from what we can see when we look out into space, into the night sky that has captivated our species since we evolved the eyes and minds to ponder it. We are very fortunate that it is possible to see the stars through Earth's atmosphere, and that it is nowadays possible for us to build telescopes capable of analysing starlight and distinguishing different objects in the night sky, whether from Earth's surface or from satellites in orbit. We now know that these points of light aren't all the same sort of thing, and they aren't all the same distance from us, as if painted onto a spherical backdrop.

The most distant objects we can see with our best equipment are about 13 billion lightyears away. A lightyear is just a measure of distance that corresponds to how far light can travel in a year. Nothing travels faster than light, and you can see from the time it takes between striking a match and the light reaching your eye (seemingly no time at all) just how fast light travels; for context, it takes light eight minutes to reach Earth from the Sun, several million miles away. That's fast! But astronomy is the science that most blurs the distinction between space and time. If light from a distant object has travelled 13 billion lightyears to reach us, it must have set off on its journey 13 billion years ago. Hence, the deeper we look into space, the further we look back in time. The farthest objects we can see existed just a few hundred million years after the universe began, which our best measurements tell us was 13.7 billion years ago.

How do we measure such vast times and distances? It's only possible because of a type of variable star whose brightness is proportional to the rate at which it flashes. Measure this rate, and we know how bright it really is. Then compare this to the apparent brightness and, because sources of light that are farther away appear less bright, we can work out its distance. Spotting these variable stars in other galaxies allowed us to work out how far away they are, and confirm that they weren't just clusters of stars within our own galaxy. Knowing the distance of those galaxies then allowed scientists to calibrate other methods of measuring even greater distances to the furthest, earliest galaxies that we can see. If that particular kind of variable star didn't exist, we'd probably have no idea how large or old the visible universe is.

When we look far away in the universe, we always look into the past, but it is reasonable to assume that the universe has roughly the same overall structure now as it had when light from objects a few billion lightyears away or less set off on its incredible journey across the depths of space and time to reach its destination at a human eye or telescope. That's amazing when you think about it! Millions or billions of years of travel, and me or my telescope is its destination! We need very powerful telescopes to look into the very deep past; some of them use light that our eyes can see, whilst others use other parts of the electromagnetic spectrum. That means other forms of light such as radio waves or x-rays, which we can't detect with our eyes. It's incredible that, somehow, we have been able to develop technologies here on our little planet that allow us to see objects so immensely far away and come to understand the stars, without having physically travelled further than our own Moon. It's only possible at all because the universe is mostly empty space, through which light is able to travel at the greatest possible speed.

Within this void, what we see on the largest scales are vast structures – an enormous web of galaxy clusters all linked up together. Quite why the universe is structured like this we don't know, nor whether the web is of a finite size or infinite in extent. The galaxy clusters each contain between dozens and thousands of galaxies, which each contain millions or billions of stars, each of which is a nuclear fusion reactor pouring out light as a by-product of fusing together atoms to make heavier ones. What holds all this together – the clusters, superclusters, galaxies and stars – is the same force that holds my feet on the floor, or this sheet of paper I'm writing on onto my desk. It's the force we know as 'gravity', and it acts between any two objects with mass. The more massive an object – basically, the more physical material it contains – the stronger the pull of its gravity. The pull that an object experiences in any given place is known as the object's 'weight', which depends on its mass but also on the mass and distance of other gravitationally attractive objects nearby. The fact that you and I have weight is largely due to the Earth's gravitational tug; on the Moon we would each have the same mass as we do on Earth, but our weight would be less because the Moon's gravity is less. In the empty void of space, far from stars and planets, we would still have mass but would be weightless.

So, because you and I both have mass, we both exert a gravitational attraction that is at this moment pulling us towards each other. However, we don't experience this attraction because that force of gravity is miniscule compared to the force of gravity from the Earth – which is much, much more massive than you or I – pulling us down. That in turn is much smaller than the force of the Sun's gravity pulling us – and the whole Earth – towards it, or the force of the neighbouring stars and galaxies pulling us towards them. That's why Earth's in orbit around the sun (a way of saying that it's trapped by the Sun's gravity) and the Sun is in orbit around the centre of our galaxy.

The odd thing about gravity is that it always attracts, never repels. Why, then, don't we get pulled as a planet straight towards the Sun? Well, if the Earth started off as stationary, that's exactly what would happen. But for an object that is already moving in a direction other than directly towards the centre of gravity, gravity can act to change the object's direction, rather than pulling it straight inwards. The Sun's gravity, then, causes the Earth to constantly change direction as it goes past the Sun, creating a near-circular orbit. The best way to think about gravity is this: imagine space (and time) as a big sheet of thick material. Now stretch that sheet out at the corners and place a big, heavy object in the middle. The object creates a big dip. If you place a smaller object – a tennis ball, say – stationary at the edge of the sheet, it will just roll down to the centre, as if attracted towards the heavy object there. But set the tennis ball rolling around the edge of the sheet and it won't roll down to the middle but spiral round and round. The ball is in orbit, and if there wasn't any friction on the sheet to slow it down it would remain in orbit indefinitely.

In this example, space time is imagined as the two-dimensional surface of a sheet. In the real universe, the same ideas hold except that the 'sheet' is now four-dimensional (including time), which is much harder to picture! When objects exert or experience gravity, the mass of each is essentially the same as the size of the 'dent' that it makes in this four-dimensional sheet, and the bigger the dent, the more likely other objects are to roll towards it. So it is that Earth orbits our Sun – falling towards its dent – the Sun orbit's the galaxy's centre of mass, and the galaxy orbits the centre of its local cluster of galaxies. Gravity rules!

Except that that's not the whole of the story. I mentioned that the universe is 13.7 billion years old. We know this because at the moment everything in the universe is accelerating outwards from the centre, like the debris flying out in all directions from giant explosion. Tracing back the motion of everything we can see in the universe – using those variable stars I mentioned before to calibrate our measurements – we find that it all meets up at a single point in space and time 13.7 billion years ago. That's where everything began (according to our best knowledge at the moment), at the moment of the so-called 'Big Bang'. We can be pretty sure about the fact that space and time as we know them began at the Big Bang; what we're not certain about at all is what came 'before' the Big Bang (though notions of 'before' don't make much sense when time itself hadn't yet begun!). Time and space began there – it's not just that things in space are expanding outwards, like a balloon being blown gradually bigger within an atmosphere of air. Space itself is expanding, as is time. Time can only go in one direction because it's being pushed forwards by that first Big Bang, just as the horizons of space are being pushed forwards.

Yet for all that we've been able to intuit so far, there's still a lot we don't know about the large-scale universe, even after the Big Bang. For one thing, I said that the universe is accelerating outwards. If you think about it, that's not what you'd expect from an explosion (indeed, when the term 'Big Bang' was jokingly coined, nobody knew that the universe was accelerating). You'd expect exploding material to be forced outwards very quickly at first, but then slow down as time goes on and it gets further away from the centre of the explosion, until the dust settles and the explosion has stopped. For an explosion on Earth, that would be because of air resistance and other things getting in the way; in space, it would be the force of gravity pulling everything back together again that stopped the explosion. Maybe gravity would be strong enough to pull everything back, eventually, to a single point again. There is a theory that the universe is undergoing an infinite series of expansions and contractions so that instead of a Big Bang there was just a 'big bounce' when it previously shrank down to a point before expanding again. Maybe time even goes backwards during the contraction phases! At the very least, even if gravity wasn't strong enough to do this, you'd think that the scattering debris would cease to increase in speed and settle into a constant velocity. This is a natural consequence of the conservation of energy. To get faster requires more energy; if energy is constant in the universe (and all our experiments suggest that it is), everything can't be getting faster and faster indefinitely! It has to stop accelerating when it stops gaining energy, which is to say just after the initial explosion.

But that's not what we see. Instead, measurements of distant objects – whose speed relative to us can be worked out from how much their light has been 'stretched' on its way to us through space – reveal that the universe's expansion is still accelerating, billions of years after the Big Bang, as if there were some other, unknown source of energy or force pushing the whole thing outwards ever faster. This energy has to come from somewhere, we don't know where. It's been dubbed 'dark energy' because its origin is mysterious and unknown (dark). This is perhaps the most intractable problem in cosmology today.

A second problem is that when we look at stars orbiting the centres of distant galaxies, they seem to be doing so faster than what our theories of gravity predict, as if there was extra matter in those galaxies that we can't see, producing a deeper dent in the space-time fabric than we expect. This has been called 'dark matter' because it, too, is mysterious and invisible. Perhaps it's just a lot of dead remains of stars that have run out of fuel and stopped shining, but that doesn't square with how much material ought to be in stars, given our measurements of what was in the early universe. Perhaps, then, it's some other form of matter that light doesn't get stopped by or interact with, so that we can't see it in the early universe and we can't see it now. We don't know, though many people are looking.

Another possibility that might have occurred to you is that we've simply got our gravity calculations wrong: maybe the force of gravity between stars and galaxies isn't as simple to understand as we think. Our theories and measurements of gravity come from observations of things here on Earth and in its surroundings. Perhaps we are wrong to assume that gravity works in the same way out in the depths of space and time; perhaps there isn't any dark energy or dark matter at all. In any case, what we can be certain of is that there are phenomena at large in the universe that we humans simply don't yet (and perhaps can't?) understand – at least, not from the vantage point of this special little watery rock we call Earth.

So, there we have it – our structure so far. A universe that is a web of superclusters and clusters of galaxies, which are each clusters of stars – usually arranged either as a spiral or an ellipse (cigar-shaped) with a 'black hole' in the centre, like a spider at the centre of each galactic web. A black hole is nothing to be frightened about – it's just what's left over when a particularly big star runs out of fuel and implodes. It's black because its gravity is so strong that even light cannot escape it, but as long as material doesn't get too close to the 'hole' in space-time, it won't get sucked in but continue to orbit as if it were just orbiting a very large mass, such as the star that originally imploded (whose mass will stay the same when it becomes a black hole).

Before we get down to the scale of stars like our own Sun and planets like ours, we need to leap from the very big to the very small. That's because our planet and all the biology on it – and, yes, you and I – are all much more complicated than stars and galaxies. They're made up almost entirely of very light-weight chemical elements: hydrogen (the very lightest of all) and helium.

It's fusing hydrogen atoms together to make helium that makes the stars shine, as this process releases energy and that energy is manifested as light. But we're made of a lot of more complicated elements – mostly carbon and oxygen but also phosphorous, iron, calcium and a lot of other things besides. It's only by looking down to the level of the very small that we've been able to understand what makes these heavier elements different from each other, and how they formed in the first place.

The great theoretical triumph of twentieth-century physics was what's known as the Standard Model of particle physics. In fact, this theory has been such a triumph that a lot of physicists spend their time devising theories and performing experiments using huge apparatus to try to break it and find a still better theory beyond it that might solve some of the gaps in our knowledge. So far, this has been to no avail. These experiments include the Large Hadron Collider in Switzerland, and involve crashing particles together at very high energies to smash them apart into more fundamental particles.

Such experiments have shown that there is a hierarchy of particle matter. All the physical 'stuff' of the universe around us is made of chemical elements; this we have known for centuries. Particle physics tells us that different elements differ because they have different combinations of fundamental particles within them. All are made up of atoms, each of which has a central heavy core – the 'nucleus' – surrounded by a fuzzy cloud of electrons, which are very lightweight negatively charged particles. The electrons are thought to be fundamental, which means that they can't be broken up into anything smaller. The nucleus, though, is composed of 'protons' with positive charge and 'neutrons' with no charge. In a neutral atom, the number of electrons is equal to the number of protons, and it's this number that determines which element it is. Hydrogen has just one proton – which it why it's so light – whereas helium has two, carbon six, oxygen eight and so on up to the heaviest known elements, which can have as many as 120 protons per nucleus.

The protons and neutrons themselves are not fundamental; they are made of two types of fundamental 'quark' known as 'up' and 'down' quarks. There are also other types of quark that make up other forms of matter that don't form part of our stable, everyday world. Other fundamental particles include neutrinos (not to be confused with neutrons) which are released in nuclear fusion reactions such as those taking place in the Sun all the time. There are millions passing through you every second, but you wouldn't know it because they hardly ever interact with 'normal' matter.

I mentioned before how gravity is king on large scales in the universe. But at the small scales of atoms and nuclei, gravity is negligible, it's so weak. That's because the force of gravity depends upon an object's mass, and fundamental particles have very little mass indeed. So it's not gravity that glues quarks together to form protons and neutrons; that's something called the 'strong nuclear force', which is incredibly strong over very short distances, but becomes very weak very quickly when objects move away from one another – it therefore effectively only applies between objects that are very close together. There's also such thing as a 'weak nuclear force' – it's 'weak' compared to the strong force (a million times weaker, in fact) but still much stronger than gravity on these small scales – which controls the radioactive decay of atoms.

Then there's the electromagnetic force, the fourth of the four fundamental forces in the universe. On sub-atomic scales, this force ranks in between the strong and weak forces in terms of strength, but because it acts between electrically charged objects it's also an important force on much larger scales such as that of the everyday world that you and I live in. Many fundamental particles have charge – electrons are 'negative', protons are made up of quarks that are 'positive' overall – and the electromagnetic force causes oppositely charged objects to attract one another and similarly charged objects to repel. That's what keeps electrons in orbit around the positive nucleus of an atom. It's the same force that makes North and South poles on magnets attract one another, but I've not got space to go into how magnetism works here, fascinating as it is!

The electromagnetic force tries to push protons apart in each atomic nucleus, which remember is composed of a number of protons and neutrons depending on which element it is – and it's to keep the nucleus together that there have to be neutrons as well as protons in all but the smallest nuclei. The neutrons have no electric charge, but their presence increases the strength of the strong nuclear force holding the nucleus together, compensating the electromagnetic repulsion.

It's a fine balancing act in every nucleus; if there are too many protons the nucleus can be unstable and break apart. We're extremely fortunate that it's possible for the two forces to balance out at all, enabling heavier elements than hydrogen (a single proton and single electron) to form. The elements that have unstable nuclei liable to break apart into smaller ones tend to be quite 'heavy elements', meaning that the nuclei contain lots of protons and neutrons. The most famous of these is uranium, and these unstable heavy elements are said to be 'radioactive' because samples of them actively emit particles as the nuclei break down, particles we refer to as 'radiation'.

The three forces that are relevant on sub-atomic scales – 'strong nuclear', 'weak nuclear' and 'electromagnetic' – are all mediated by force-carrier particles that essentially travel back and forth between interacting particles and carry the force between them. The force-carrier for the electromagnetic force is the photon, and it's photons that make up what we experience as light. They travel at the greatest possible speed in the universe – the 'speed of light' – and a ray of photons is known as an electromagnetic wave, which is the same thing as a beam of light. This beam isn't like a beam of ordinary matter, like a long stream of water being ejected from a hose for example, because it behaves both as a particle and as a wave at the same time, but we won't go into that just now.

So why was it necessary to go into all this detail about tiny scales much smaller than the width of a hair, to tell the story of the creation of the universe and the

Earth? Because it's what happens at these scales that determined how the Earth could form, and indeed what happened in the earliest moments of the universe's existence. Indeed, we now have all the tools in place to create a sketch of the creation of the universe, galaxy, solar system and planet on which we live, as well as how organisms themselves came about, from a physical perspective.

At the time of the Big Bang, the universe wasn't very big at all – it came from an infinitely small extent, and very, very rapidly ballooned outwards. The earliest time we can look back to is known as the 'Planck time' (after a very famous theoretical physicist), which was 5×10^{-44} seconds after the Big Bang – that's 0.5 seconds, with another 43 zeros after the decimal point: a tiny, tiny instant of time. All we can say about the universe at this time is that it was a formless collection of 'primeval black holes' containing no matter at all. All the four fundamental forces – gravity, strong, weak and electromagnetic – were unified at this time. By 10^{-36} seconds, gravity – the weakest force but with the longest range – had separated out from the others, then the strong force separated out, then about 10^{-11} seconds after the Big Bang quarks formed. Protons and neutrons formed from these at 0.001 seconds, then neutrinos after 0.1 seconds. Phew! An awful lot happening in just a tenth of a second! By this time, an extremely rapid expansion of the universe had occurred, which meant that it went from essentially nothing to around 1 metre in diameter. For the next 13.7 billion years it has continued to expand, more slowly, so that the presently observable universe is many trillions of metres across.

Throughout all this expansion, as well as getting bigger the universe has also been cooling down: that is to say, the particles of matter that it contains have been jiggling about, on average, ever more slowly and less energetically. It's only when matter cools down sufficiently that it's able to accumulate into larger structures – much like steam cooling down to condense into water droplets. When a material is hot, all the particles zip around quickly, and if they crash into each other they tend to ricochet apart again; as they slow down, they're more likely to stick together. The early universe, say from about 1 second after the Big Bang onwards, was dominated by radiation – light – of a very high energy indeed, and particles such as electrons, neutrinos and photons moving at very high speed in a seething soup. After about 5000 years, though, the universe had cooled to a relatively cool 9000 degrees Celsius, and matter began to dominate over radiation – that is to say, there was more energy in the form of physical stuff than in the form of light. That's because the expansion of the universe stretched out the light waves over time, so that the wave length – akin to the distance between consecutive wave crests or wave troughs in a water wave – increased. Light with a higher wavelength is less energetic, so takes up a smaller proportion of the universe's energy.

By now, protons and neutrons were able to combine to form the first atomic nuclei, because they were moving slowly enough. Naturally, hydrogen and helium (the smallest nuclei) were the easiest to form. About 300 000 years after the Big Bang, when the temperature dropped to around 3000 degrees, the positive protons in these nuclei could capture negative electrons, forming the first neutral atoms – the building blocks of all the material we know in the world around us. Unhampered by electrons' interference, light rays were able for the first time to move freely from this point, so that the universe changed from opaque to transparent! The resulting light – known as 'Cosmic Microwave Background radiation' – is still travelling freely across the universe and, amazingly, is still detectable today, coming from all directions in the sky at once. It was discovered by accident in the 1960s when two researchers couldn't get rid of the background hiss in the microwave part of the electromagnetic spectrum they were detecting with their powerful new radio telescope. They cleaned the telescope and removed some pigeons that had been nesting in it (radio telescopes are very large, more like huge satellite dishes in appearance than optical telescopes you might be more familiar with) but the signal wouldn't go away. Its remarkable smoothness, the same whichever way we look, tells us that the early universe was also very smooth and uniform.

That's not the universe we know and love today! Our universe is mostly empty space, but dotted with stars in galaxies of all shapes and sizes. What happened? Well, the Big Bang only created two types of chemical element: hydrogen (a proton and an electron, sometimes with a neutron or two) and helium (two protons and one or two neutrons orbited by two electrons). Although the early universe was very, very uniform, there were tiny differences in the density of the hydrogen and the helium from one place to the next. The very slightly denser places then attracted more matter towards themselves under gravity, causing the matter in the universe eventually – over a long period of time – to begin to coalesce in these places, making lumps that would become the galaxies.

In the fullness of time, the matter in these proto-galaxies became so dense in places that gravity began to push the hydrogen atoms very close together indeed, so much so that they began to fuse into helium. The point at which a cloud of matter begins nuclear fusion is the ignition of a star. The furthest galaxy that our telescopes can see contains many of these very early stars, and because it is so far away we know that we are seeing this galaxy as it was just 780 million years after the Big Bang. That may not sound a small amount of time, until you realise that it means we're looking back around 13 billion years from the present day.

If all that stars did was convert hydrogen into helium like this, the universe would be a very dull place, and you and I wouldn't exist. Hydrogen and helium are colourless, odourless gasses that no form of life could ever conceivably consist of. Fortunately, though, all stars go through several stages during their life-cycles, and helium is far from the end of the story. The exact details of a star's life story depend on the mass of the star – the amount of matter that it formed from in the first place –

but I'll try to describe the evolution of some typical examples.

A low-mass star (less than or roughly equal to the mass of our Sun) won't do for making heavier elements, as this sort of star only has various phases of hydrogen and helium 'burning' as it's called – the star isn't on fire in the everyday sense, you understand, but looks as if it is because nuclear fusion releases a lot of heat and light. These stars end up bulging out to a huge size then shrinking down to a gradually cooling core known as a 'white dwarf' which after a long, slow death will eventually go out. That is indeed to be the fate of our own Sun, in several billion years' time when it runs out of hydrogen and then of helium.

Bigger stars have much more interesting life-cycles. After a star's hydrogen has mostly run out there tends to be an awful lot of helium around, and most stars are massive enough to fuse the helium nuclei together to form carbon and oxygen. Carbon has six protons per atom and each carbon nucleus formed therefore requires three helium nuclei to combine (each of which has two protons) whereas making oxygen requires four because it has eight protons per nucleus, so the oxygen usually forms by helium combining with carbon that's already been produced. You might be wondering why two helium nuclei don't first combine to form an element with four protons per nucleus, rather than jumping straight to carbon with six. Well, initially they do, and that element is beryllium. The trouble is that the form of beryllium this produces, known as beryllium-8 because it has four protons and four neutrons (so eight 'nucleons') in its nucleus, is very unstable. In fact it's so unstable that it breaks apart again into helium nuclei in less than a trillionth of a second! This is a problem, and indeed it's a much bigger problem than the story I've given you so far might lead you to believe.

I said that three helium nuclei could fuse to form carbon. But it's very, very unlikely that three such nuclei would happen to collide together at exactly the same time, even in a very dense environment such as that of a hot star. It's much easier for two helium nuclei to combine than three – so you need two to combine first to form beryllium, then another to combine with this to form carbon. Except that I've just told you that beryllium-8 is very unstable, and it doesn't last long enough for the third nucleus to have time to be added in to form stable carbon. That's because for the resulting carbon nucleus to be stable and not break apart again itself, there needs to be time for any extra energy associated with the combined mass of beryllium and helium nuclei being very slightly more than that of the carbon nucleus to escape (mass energy can be converted to light energy in extreme places such as stars). When scientists first came across this conundrum, it seemed impossible that carbon could form from helium in stars! That would put a brake on the creation of other, heavier elements – and would mean that we, and all other carbon-based life, could not exist.

Indeed, scientists worked out – this was in the late 1940s – that the only way carbon and heavier elements could exist, given that nothing other than stars is known in which the conditions are extreme enough to produce them – is if a particular hypothetical physical arrangement of a carbon-12 nucleus were to exist such that the energy of this nucleus was exactly the same as the combined energy of the beryllium nucleus and helium nucleus needed to combine to produce it. Then, it was just possible that the beryllium nucleus could survive without decaying for just about long enough to form carbon. This seemed a very unlikely possibility: there is no 'a priori' reason why a carbon nucleus of just the right structure and energy for this to work should happen to exist. Nor was there any evidence at the time that it did exist.

But experiments were run, possible carbon structures were investigated and, amazingly, it was found that this particular arrangement of carbon does indeed exist, with exactly the right mass, and beryllium-8 does indeed survive just long enough to combine with helium to produce it in stars. An incredible coincidence, without which the universe we know could never have existed! It was also a triumph for the 'scientific method': an observation had been made (in this case the fact that anything heavier than helium exists), a prediction was formulated (that the correct 'excited' state of carbon must exist) and an experiment was made to test and prove the hypothesis.

Why am I telling you all this? To illustrate just how amazing and incredibly improbable it is that matter heavier than helium exists at all. Now that the star can form carbon, if it is heavy enough (and our Sun isn't), the process of stellar evolution can continue in a similar vein for other elements. The star goes through a sequence of phases in which chemical elements that it has already manufactured through nuclear fusion can be combined with other elements to form heavier ones. This nuclear fusion releases energy, which the star uses to remain hot and bright. Elements are produced with more and more protons and neutrons in the nucleus in a sequence of different 'burning' phases, until the star pummels its lighter elements together to form iron-56, which has 28 protons and 28 neutrons per nucleus.

Once the star runs out of elements lighter than iron, though, it hits upon a problem. Iron sits at the bottom of an energy 'well' in that it possesses the least energy per nucleon (proton or neutron) of any nucleus. Fuse elements lighter than iron together, and energy is released to keep the star in business, but to produce elements heavier than iron, energy has to be put in. In other words, iron is not a good fuel for nuclear fusion, and without nuclear fusion, the star will die. This is very bad news for the star: once it is mostly iron, its energy reserves are expended and it can no longer produce the light and heat energy necessary to resist the inward pull of its own gravity and keep itself aloft. The star collapses under the force of its own weight – and implodes. The implosion of the core releases energy that causes an explosion of the outer layers of the star, and a huge amount of light is produced. This explosion is known as a 'supernova', and it's incredibly bright. Indeed, a supernova can be so bright that it outshines an entire galaxy – but only for a few weeks before it fades away.

What remains behind after a supernova has occurred is a lot of dust – literally, stardust – containing a whole mixture of elements, including all the elements heavier than iron ever made. Because energy has to be put in to form them, they can only be produced in very energetic explosions like that of the supernova. Our bodies contain (in small amounts) all sorts of elements heavier than iron, which we couldn't live without. That means that you and I are literally made of stardust formed in supernova explosions, as well as lighter elements made during the active lifetime of massive stars that were active in the early stages of the universe's history.

The supernova also leaves behind a very dense, massive remnant with a very strong gravitational pull: a neutron star in which all the electrons and protons have been squeezed together to form neutrons, or – if the star was really very big before it collapsed – a black hole. But most of the gas and dust produced by the supernova escapes the gravitational tug of the remnant core and drifts off to form part of the swamp of gas floating in empty space called the 'interstellar medium', enriching it with heavy elements. In time, this medium's denser parts collapse to form new stars, which still have lots of hydrogen and helium – the interstellar medium is packed with those elements – but also traces of the heavier elements from the supernova dust.

Our Sun is one of those newer stars that formed from the remnants of older generations of stars mixed in with lighter elements left over from the Big Bang. Our planet, along with the other seven planets in the Solar

System and myriad smaller objects, formed from the same cloud of gas and dust that formed the Sun, but further out from the dense centre of the Solar System. Before the Sun grew dense enough to ignite, the whole system would have been a diffuse disc orbiting the Sun, but over time the material had clumped together through particle collisions to clear most of the space in this disc and leave only a few, much bigger pieces of material. Most of them orbit in the same plane, the original plane of the disc from which they formed, with each planet making a full circuit around the Sun in the course of that planet's year.

The rules of orbital motion mean that planets further away from the Sun orbit with a longer year, at a lower speed and with a greater distance to travel, than planets closer in. The outer planets are also much cooler, which means that they are composed mostly of gas – a lot of hydrogen and helium again, amongst other things – and are on the whole larger; the inner planets like our own Earth are closer to the Sun and therefore warmer, which means that lighter gasses like those long ago 'boiled off' and mostly heavier elements remain. That's why they're relatively small and rocky; the bulk of the material that makes up the Earth, say, would form the centre of a planet like Jupiter but be surrounded by much larger quantities of gas.

Water's abundance on Earth is actually quite tricky to explain: it's made of hydrogen and oxygen that should have boiled off the early Earth (which used to be much hotter than it is now) yet Earth is clearly covered in the stuff! There are several theories as to how it miraculously got its water; one of the most prominent is that it arrived on icy comets, but recent analyses of the composition of comets suggest that this is unlikely and that perhaps it somehow survived from the material that first coalesced to form Earth after all. In any case, somehow this vital ingredient for life ended up dominating our planet's surface, which is most fortunate for us. None of the other planets or moons in our solar system possess water in such abundance in such an accessible form (as opposed to frozen underground or in trace amounts, like on the Moon), which is why – we think – none of them are capable of supporting biological life. The miracle of life on Earth will be the topic of the next chapter.

Our Sun is about 5 billion years old, and has about as long as this to go before it runs out of hydrogen and swells into a huge helium-burning star engulfing Mercury, Venus, Earth and possibly Mars. Earth itself is around 4.6 billion years old, and was formed during the collision of two earlier planets that merged together, their detritus forming the Moon. That explains why our Moon is so much bigger than most moons in the Solar System, which tend to be passing rocks that have strayed too close to a planet and got caught by its gravity. A 'moon' is simply an object that orbits a planet under gravity (and is natural, rather than a man-made satellite).

The gravitational tug on the collision debris as they formed is what led to the Earth and the Moon being almost perfectly spherical, and the same effect applied to all the other planets when they formed from the Solar

System's disc of gas and dust, which is why they're spherical too. The moons of other planets often have much less regular shapes, which is a sign that they didn't form at the same time as their host planets, but are more likely to be recently-captured passers-by. An interesting fact about our Moon is that it is 'tidally locked', which means that whilst it orbits the Earth every 28 days, it also rotates at the same rate, so that the same side always faces the Earth. The phase of the Moon (full, half, new) is set by how much of the Earth-facing side is lit by the Sun, which depends on the angle between the Earth, Moon and Sun and hence on the part of its 28-day orbit the Moon has reached. The 'dark side of the Moon' isn't really necessarily 'dark' at all – it's just the side that we can't see from Earth.

The Moon and its phases have had a great influence on human culture and our ability to track times and seasons before we invented writing, and it has also influenced the development of other forms of life on Earth. The Solar Eclipse – when the Moon gets in the way of the Sun and blocks its light from the perspective of Earth – and the Lunar Eclipse – when the Earth gets between the Sun and the Moon – are especially wonderful natural displays that have inspired awe and helped to nurture our human urge to discover the laws of nature since our species evolved. It's quite a miracle, though, that these eclipses can occur at all. It just so happens that for the period of human history (the blink of an eye on the timescale of the planet's history) the Moon is just the right distance from Earth that it appears to be exactly the same size as the Sun in our sky. The

Moon has been for many millennia moving away from us, so its apparent size is actually getting gradually smaller. Had our species evolved just a few million years later, the Moon would be too small in the sky to block out the Sun and cause an eclipse, and this cultural inspiration would not exist! Amazing!

That word, 'amazing', is probably as good as any to sum up the history of the universe at large to this point, from the Big Bang to the creation of the Earth and the Moon. It's a sequence of events, all of which are explicable to us only if we invoke certain 'laws of nature' (such as how gravity works) and certain fortunate coincidences (such as the existence of a specific type of carbon-12 with just the right energy). What we cannot explain through physics, though, is why such laws of nature exist in the first place, nor why such coincidences have happened. All we know is that they must exist, and must have happened, or else we wouldn't be here at all.

We'll return to the philosophical implications of this in Chapter 10. For now, though, let's have a look at the story of how life came into being. That's the subject of the next Chapter.

8

The Miracle of Life

Somewhere in this vast universe, amongst all the billions of galaxies containing billions of stars – each of which may have several planets – it is not surprising that just the right conditions arose for a new phenomenon to come into being on at least one of these planets, the phenomenon of biological life. For all we know, our Sun may be the only star to host life: the rest of those billions of billions of stars may be as silent and lifeless as so many grains of sand, like the trillions that sit beneath our oceans.

It's not miraculous that conditions are just perfect for life to exist on Earth, given that there are so many other worlds where they are not suitable (we think), and we'll come on to what makes Earth special in this respect soon. But what is miraculous is that a universe exists at all; that it has the right laws and properties to mean that stars form; that these are able to produce all sorts of chemical elements with all sorts of properties; that the stars have planets orbiting them that are so varied in composition, size and habitability; and that, given all this, our universe is capable of supporting life – at least, in this little corner of this backwater galaxy where you and I live.

Some people have tried to explain this miracle by suggesting that there is a whole 'multiverse' of different universes, each with different laws of physics and 'fundamental constants' (things like the mass of the electron and the strength of gravity) whose values we cannot explain. But that's only to defer the miracle, for if there was any hard evidence for the existence of a multiverse (which there isn't – at least not yet), one could say that it was equally a miracle that a multiverse with so many and varied universes in it existed such that in at least one corner of this multiverse there was a universe in which there was a galaxy in which there was a star around which there was a planet capable of supporting life! We could go on with this indefinitely, conjuring up imaginary 'Russian dolls' to represent bigger and bigger dimensions of reality, with the properties of each one explained by the fact that it exists amongst many others in some higher-dimensional collection. The Earth's existence is not remarkable because there are so many planets in the galaxy, which isn't remarkable because there are so many galaxies in the universe, and so on, but eventually we must reach the ultimate scale on which there is only one thing – universe, multiverse, multiverse of multiverses or whatever – the existence of which is indeed remarkable.

Personally, I don't think it's helpful to get ourselves tangled up thinking about multiverses whose existence we can't explain, to repeat what I said in Chapter 7. So for now, let's assume that there's just our universe. We'll just have to accept, for now, that it has certain properties and constants that allow physical matter to exist in the form we know and love it. Perhaps these constants and properties have been tweaked somehow to make them just right; perhaps they couldn't be any different: putting a mathematical number on something, like the size of the electron's charge or the strength of gravity for instance, tempts us to imagine that that number could be different – slightly higher, or slightly lower, for example – because we're so used to counting things with numbers. But there's no reason to think that it really could. Some numbers, like π (pi) are just ratios whose exact values depend on how we count numbers, and can never change or be different to what they are unless we change the number line we use to count. All the fundamental constants of the universe might be like that: they are as they are because they couldn't be anything else.

But let's not worry too much about that. The scene is set – somehow – the planets are formed around countless stars, and on at least one of those planets something arises called life. Why is life so important? Because, for all the planets, stars, moons, asteroids, nebulae, galaxies, black holes, neutron stars and numerous other physical things that exist out there in the great, wide universe, there is nothing so complicated, intricate and wonderful as life. That our own planet is perfect for life is no surprise to us, because we could only exist on a planet perfect for life – which is why, incidentally, though we don't know whether rudimentary life of some sort exists on other planets in our vicinity for certain, it is very, very unlikely that intelligent life like ours is very common in the universe. Earth is too perfect for life for us to happen to exist here if we could just have easily have evolved on more numerous less-than-perfect alternatives such as Mars.

What is it that makes our planet so perfect? There's a whole list of things, of which I'll give a few. Firstly, there's our star, the Sun. Stars can have average temperatures across a whole range of possible values: some are very hot, some are comparatively cold. Our Sun is a 'goldilocks' star: it's neither too hot nor too cold. Very hot stars release lots of dangerous ionising radiation that could destroy all life, and they 'live fast, die young' so would probably not last long enough for very complex lifeforms like human beings to evolve on planets orbiting them. Colder stars can't provide enough energy to even their innermost planets for life as we know it to exist: photosynthesis, for example, wouldn't work with a very low-energy star. Furthermore, our Sun doesn't vary much in its output – it would be very difficult for life to get a foothold around a star that kept getting brighter and dimmer, as some do, plunging its planets from freezing cold to boiling hot all the time.

Another important factor is our Moon. That, too, is a stable presence, and we're very fortunate that it formed in the way it did (see Chapter 7). The Moon is not just a pretty face in the night sky; it's acted, over the course of billions of years, like a magnet for incoming space rocks, big enough to hoover many of them up before they reached Earth or to deflect them away. That means mass-extinctions from asteroid impacts are less likely than they would be without it. Our near-neighbour planet Jupiter, too, because it's such a huge planet with a massive gravitational punch, acts like a cosmic big brother to defend us from many interstellar objects that come hurtling towards the Solar System, drawing them away to itself. It's a fortunate thing, in other words, that our planet's not alone in orbiting the Sun.

Earth itself is in a good place in the Solar System, too. There's another sort of 'goldilocks zone' which for any star is the region between orbits that are too close to the star (where planets get frazzled like Mercury) and those that are too far away (where they get frozen like Neptune). Our planet sits in just the right place so that one essential ingredient of life as we know it – water – is liquid and accessible on the surface, so long as another essential ingredient – the atmosphere – is present. This atmosphere contains 'greenhouse gasses' such as water vapour and carbon dioxide that trap heat from the Sun so that it cannot escape straight back into space. Without them, the average surface temperature of the planet would be about minus 18 degrees Celsius, rather than the plus 14 degrees we enjoy now! Some of these gasses were put there by life itself, in a beautiful natural interaction whereby primitive lifeforms began to develop and change the world around themselves to make it more suitable for that same life to proliferate. The presence of life itself has hence made our world warmer over many millennia, at a very gradual pace that allowed life to slowly adapt and flourish in the changing conditions. You certainly wouldn't want the effect to go too far or too fast: Venus is very similar in size to Earth but has an atmosphere that is 96% carbon dioxide, and its 'runaway' greenhouse effect means that the average surface temperature is an insufferable 464 degrees Celsius!

The presence of water is vital for nearly all life we know of, and somehow this precious substance became abundant on Earth. We also benefit from the presence of volcanoes on our planet, which allow minerals from deep underground to be 'recycled' onto Earth's surface, again a boon for life. Earth also has a natural sort of force-field caused by the magnetism of its inner metals, which exerts a magnetic force to deflect a lot of the harmful radiation that arrives from our own Sun or from the universe beyond. That's important if emerging life isn't to be periodically sterilised by bursts of deadly particles streaming towards Earth. Finally, we can add to these beneficial properties of the Earth and the Sun that they are both in a relatively quiet corner of the galaxy, not towards the centre where there are lots of potentially very dangerous things going on.

It's taken 4.6 billion years for the plants, animals, bacteria, fungi and other less visible living things that inhabit our world today to get to where they are now. They weren't just placed here overnight. In fact, all life evolved according to an important law of biology, a bit like the laws of physics that determined the evolution of the universe at large. Indeed, it arises as a natural implication of such physical laws. This biological law was discovered in the mid-nineteenth century, by the very famous naturalist Charles Darwin. It's called the Principle of Evolution by Natural Selection, and it's what led to all the diverse life we know and love today.

Evolution was known about long before Darwin – all 'evolution' really means is 'development over time', and we knew that living beings around us didn't stay fixed for all time. It was most obvious in species of animal and plant that humans had domesticated, such as the dog and the horse, because we knew that by 'selective breeding' – that is, by choosing offspring with desired characteristics like friendliness, speed or the ability to endure harsh weather and allowing only those individuals to breed – we had radically changed the appearance and characteristics of those species over the centuries. A Jack Russell dog looks very different to a wild wolf, for instance. People had known this for centuries, whether they were educated or lived on the land alongside the animals in question, even if they didn't call it 'evolution'. But Darwin for the first time identified the mechanism through which evolution occurs in nature, without man's hand to guide it.

'Natural Selection' as a phrase just means 'selective breeding, but not by humans'. When humans select offspring with certain traits they make a conscious decision – 'I want a dog that can run fast to help me herd my sheep', or 'I want a strain of wheat that is easy to digest'. The first farmers practised selection by weeding out plants they didn't like and allowing those they did like to grow without competition. That meant that only the desirable plants, like edible grains, had the chance to reproduce and become more abundant over time, in the area where humans practised cultivation. Some individuals amongst the edible plants might have more accessible seeds than others, and at some point somebody decided to start gathering the seeds and planting them, thus causing similar plants to grow. Then, they realised that if they planted seeds from individual plants with certain characteristics – those from the most edible sorts of wheat, say – those seeds would grow into individuals that were likely to share the same characteristics – to be easy to eat, say. You can see how, over the course of many generations, by selecting seed from the 'best' plants to sow, humans ended up with very desirable crops, quite artificially, instead of the random assortment of plants that might naturally grow. They had selected for characteristics that they desired.

Natural Selection works in the same way, except that there's no human making conscious decisions. Instead, it's the suitability of an individual to its particular surroundings that makes it more or less likely to be 'selected' to be able to produce offspring and pass on its characteristics to future generations. A wolf with slightly longer legs, for instance, might be able to run faster, and so be more likely to be a successful hunter and survive to reproduce and pass on its long-legs characteristics to its pups.

What Darwin didn't know, and we now do, is that all of this (both human selection and Natural Selection) takes place because of genes. An organism always passes on some of its genes, which are a sort of code that determines its physical characteristics, to its offspring. Most of our genes are therefore inherited from our parents (which is why a monkey can't give birth to a goldfish) but random genetic mutations frequently occur and corrupt some of the genes, which means that an offspring's genes are always slightly different to those of its parents. This, coupled with the fact that for many lifeforms (and all the complicated ones like mammals) there are two parents, each giving half their genes to their children, means that every individual is genetically extinct ('clones' such as strawberry plants are an exception, but I won't go into that here). That gives every individual the possibility of having slightly better or worse characteristics than its neighbours, and allows Natural Selection to do its work.

Some of the wolf's pups might inherit the gene for longer legs, some might not, and some might happen to have a random genetic mutation that gives them shorter legs, or a longer tail, or a different colour, or a whole host of other possibilities. These genetic mutations are key to evolution. If they give rise to traits that happen to make an individual better suited to its surroundings, that individual is more likely than its neighbours to survive and reproduce, and pass on this genetic material to others. If an organism's genes give it a slight disadvantage, on the other hand – such as a wolf having shorter legs and being slower – it will be less likely to survive or to impress a mate, so that genetic material will be lost when it dies without offspring.

In this way, species adapt to suit their environment, which is why birds on predator-free tropical islands lose the ability to fly over many generations – because they don't need to – whilst many European songbirds have evolved the ability to fly thousands of miles so as to be able to escape harsh winters. It's all happened naturally, through the selection of 'good' genes, and has led to the development of millions of species each with their own special abilities that suit their particular living conditions. What's more, evolution is always going on – the natural world is never static. When something changes in the environment – it starts getting warmer, say, or a new predator evolves and starts hunting things – this puts new pressures on existing species and causes them to change to suit the changed surroundings. Species adapt and diversify, with Natural Selection automatically acting to favour newly-desirable traits.

It didn't have to be this way for life to exist in some form, but it did have to be this way for complicated and diverse lifeforms like human beings to arise. Without Natural Selection, there would be no imperative for the first, primitive life – which was very simple – to gradually get more and more complicated over billions of years. By using genetic code that is subject to occasional random mutations, and allowing the possibility of two parents producing each offspring, life has evolved in a way that can give rise to very complicated beings, diversifying life on Earth and allowing it to survive in almost every environment from scorching deserts to deep-sea vents. In longer-lived species such as our own the process is lengthy and it can take millennia to evolve adaptations to new environmental conditions – lighter skin in cooler climates, for instance. In short-lived species like bacteria, evolution can happen almost before our eyes. That's why many bacteria have evolved resistance to our antibiotic drugs designed to kill them, over the course of just a few decades.

Life hasn't always been like this; it's taken billions of years to reach present-day levels of resilience and diversity for life on Earth. The first lifeforms appeared about 4 billion years ago, only 600 million years after the planet itself formed (which tells us that either life is probably very abundant elsewhere in the universe or that Earth really is the perfect place for it). The exact point at which mixtures of chemicals that were the building blocks of primitive life can be said to have become 'alive' is a matter of debate, and we aren't sure exactly where the first life came about. A theory that was popular for a long time was that it was in deep-sea hydrothermal vents, but scientists have since made other suggestions and it could have been anywhere from deserts to the Arctic conditions of the ancient polar regions. At the moment we can't tell for sure, but we do know that life would need the right mixture of chemical ingredients and the right environmental conditions to coincide somehow in order to make the first being, and that this being must have been very simple indeed by the standards of modern-day nature.

The key to our understanding of where life came from in the first place lies more in chemistry than biology: the biology comes later, once a 'biosphere' had been established. The first lifeforms were nothing more than tiny bags of chemicals (which we still are today, I suppose, albeit much bigger and more complicated ones) capable of fulfilling what we regard as the basic criteria for being alive. You might have encountered these criteria at school in your biology lessons. I was taught them via the acronym 'MRS NERG': a living thing must be able to Move, Respire (which really means 'process chemicals' at its most basic level), Sense (so, know about or respond to its environment), use Nutrients, Excrete, Reproduce and Grow. Actually, the biology buffs tell us that this is a somewhat simplistic view of what constitutes 'life' but you get the picture. At some point the first life evolved out of not-life: a breakthrough shift from chemicals to organisms.

This might have occurred more than once, but genetic studies tell us that all life around today stems from a single common ancestor – some ancient, ancient progenitor of us all – which suggests that the spark of life didn't jump into inert matter very often and the chances of it happening were slim. What was the earliest lifeform like? Well, to be able to ancestor life as we know it today, complete with DNA codes – the 'genes' we mentioned earlier – that are essential for Natural Selection, we know that the first life must have possessed three things: a 'metabolism' to generate energy so that it could do something, a genetic code that it could use to copy itself and produce future generations, and some sort of membrane to give it shape and define it as a single being. There are a few basic elements – hydrogen, carbon, oxygen and the like – that make up these things in modern organisms, so these must have been readily available where the first life evolved. Exactly how these elements coalesced into the precursor to DNA to begin the story of life on Earth remains a mystery, and it's frankly miraculous that it ever happened at all.

From that first organism onwards, the future of genetic codes – chemical patterns – that determine each individual's features and are imperfectly passed on to successive generations during reproduction enabled Natural Selection to work its magical power on life, gradually improving, altering and generally diversifying it into millions of different species with different characteristics and habitats. If evolution has a 'purpose', that's what it is: increasing the diversity of life on Earth, and making it ever more resilient to destruction. It would be extremely difficult to kill off all life on Earth today, as there are so many species adapted to such a wide range of conditions – bacteria now live almost everywhere.

This comes as a natural consequence of the fact that organisms reproduce by copying DNA with slight variations each time, and spread out to colonise their surroundings. Such slight variations make every individual unique and slightly different, meaning that some organisms can colonise places that others cannot. Natural Selection then works on these different groups differently, making each group better-adapted to its environment, because the best-adapted individuals are more likely to survive and pass on their genes to the next generation. Eventually, the two groups become so distinct that we would class them as two different species (sometimes this point is considered to be that at which the two groups that were originally one species can no longer reproduce with each other to produce fertile offspring, though this only works for the sorts of lifeforms – like you and me – who have two parents, and isn't a catch-all definition).

That's what must have happened to the earliest life. It evolved somewhere – we don't know where, though we can guess – but as it spread out into other places it diversified and ended up splitting off into distinct species, all still simple and single-celled. The earliest life was single-celled, but eventually, an individual was created – or 'born' if you like – that had multiple cells joined together, and its offspring ended up giving rise to all the multicellular organisms – including all the plants and animals with which we are familiar every day.

The earliest lifeforms didn't breathe in oxygen (not that they had lungs anyway); to them it was poisonous, because it's a highly reactive gas. If you don't believe me, see if you can look up a video of something very flammable like hydrogen being set light to. When anything catches fire, the chemicals in that object are 'oxidising' – reacting with oxygen – and you can see the result: flames of light and heat, sometimes explosive. A lot of lifeforms were killed off by what we know as the 'Great Oxygenation Event' about 2 billion years ago. This was caused by a few individuals developing a genetic mutation that allowed them to produce oxygen, and soon enough life began to adapt to the new conditions by evolving not only to live with but actually to take advantage of the oxygen, harnessing its reactive power to do much more complicated things than lifeforms were capable of doing before. The descendants of these oxygen-loving species gave rise to plants, then animals, and eventually human beings among the animals. The sophisticated functions of our bodies – including our brains – all depend on oxygen being supplied to our comparatively sophisticated cells.

Natural Selection, gently working on tiny, random changes in the genes of individuals, has led to the amazing diversity of life we see today. 'Tiny' is an important word in that sentence. It's only very tiny changes that can be beneficial to an organism and end up getting passed on to future generations; it would be very unlikely indeed for a big change caused by a genetic mutation to be beneficial. Let me give you an example: let's return to our wolf. If a wolf that depends on chasing down its prey for its survival develops, through a random change in the DNA passed down from its parents, a slightly longer leg, that might be beneficial. But if it develops instead, through a different mutation, an extra leg, or is missing a leg entirely – much bigger physical consequences – it is likely that this will very much hamper its ability to catch its prey, and make it wholly unable to survive in the environment that its species has adapted to. That wolf is then very unlikely indeed to reproduce, and the gene for 'extra leg' or 'missing leg' gets lost, and isn't passed on to future generations – unlike the gene for slightly longer legs, which might well get passed down.

Eventually, all the wolves in that population may inherit the gene for longer legs and become faster runners, which will in turn put evolutionary pressure on the prey species to get better at running away. This whole dynamic takes place over the course of several generations. The reason why all successful genetic mutations that end up being passed on and surviving within population correspond to small changes in a species' attributes is that the species before the genetic change is already – because of previous evolution – quite well-suited to its environment. Any drastic change will almost certainly upset this suitability. So it is that evolution works little by little, generation by generation, to introduce changes. There was no sudden leap from sea-dwelling sponges (the first animals, around 700 million years ago) to fish to mammals like mankind, but a very gradual process of evolution.

How do we know all this? Without possessing a time machine, how can we work out that life evolved through Natural Selection over billions of years, rather than just appearing fully-formed as it is today? We've already seen one piece of evidence: the active manipulation of evolution by human beings to select for characteristics that we desire – and if we can do it, it can also happen naturally (albeit more slowly) by the same mechanism. But that's circumstantial evidence: it tells us that Natural Selection could occur, not that it does occur or has occurred. Fortunately, we don't need to defy the laws of physics to look into the past; we can see evidence of past aeons all around us in the world we observe today, both imprinted in its geology and written in its biology.

The fossil record is an important source of evidence. When plants and animals die, they sometimes get trapped in particular conditions – for example, an animal might fall into a peat bog, or a plant's remains may get smothered beneath layers and layers of leaves on a forest floor – in which there is not enough oxygen for the remains to rot away. In that case, these remains can be preserved, squashed beneath millions of years' worth of sediment or soil, even as the compacted material above them hardens into rock. Over time, as the Earth's continents slide around its surface (a very slow effect but one that we can measure today) and rocks rise and fall, while seas erode coastlines or retreat from rising headlands, those remains that were buried for so long can be brought back to the surface again.

At any time in Earth's history, therefore, there will be these remains – fossils – being laid down in swampy places, fossils that are millions of years old already buried deep underground where they can't be seen, and fossils just being brought to light again. In our own age, hence, scientists have discovered an analysed many thousands of fossils that constitute the preserved remains of ancient organisms. Each one can be dated from the layer of rock in which it is buried and the minerals that this rock contains. One way of dating rocks, for instance, is by looking for tiny amounts of radioactive elements in the rock, as these get less and less radioactive over time, so that the amount of radioactivity left today tells us how long ago the rocks were formed. From this, we are able to establish a picture of what sorts of organisms existed when.

There are gaps in the record (a lot of the fossils are too far from the surface for us to find them, after all) but it's frankly incredible that this should be possible at all – that the universe and its laws are such that organic material that usually rots away so quickly can be preserved in this way, and that we can date it all these years later and thereby understand our own origins! And yet it's true. That such a record existed, unbeknown to them through all the generations up to a few hundred years ago, would have astounded our ancestors. Fossils weren't discovered until the eighteenth century.

The implications of what fossils tell us for biology are equally astounding. Through the fossil record, we can piece together the evolution of all life that we know of today. The inevitable gaps have to be filled with educated guesses – hypotheses – as to what was going on, but there can be no doubt whatsoever that life has changed dramatically over time, becoming gradually more complex and diverse, leading up to the plants, animals, microbes and fungi of today. It's only through the fossil record that we know of ages when reptiles ruled the world – the dinosaurs, whose remains have now been discovered across all continents, but which were utterly unknown before the 1700s. We know also that the dinosaurs suffered three 'mass extinctions' in which nearly all species died out, only for life to spring back again in new forms – hence the 'Triassic', 'Jurassic' and 'Cretaceous' periods of dinosaur dominance.

After the extinction event that ended the Cretaceous period (which may famously have been caused by an asteroid hitting Earth) the dinosaurs' surviving species evolved into the birds and reptiles we have today, and the mammals – including, eventually, human beings – came to prominence. The story of life is

177

a wonderful pre-history, made possible only by fossils and decades or tireless research, observation and thought by palaeo-archaeologists!

There's another quirk of the laws of physics mixed in with all of this, without which life as we know it would be impossible. It's believed that all animal life began in the sea, and that the first animals to venture onto land were semi-aquatic creatures: like fish that, through random genetic mutations that enabled an individual at some point to survive for a time out of water, can also live on land. All life that we know of depends on water of some sort to exist. But if water behaved like most liquids, complex lifeforms might never have evolved – or might not have survived for very long. Most liquids get denser when they freeze. Take some mercury (well, don't – it's poisonous – but it's a liquid at room temperature), lower its temperature to below its melting point, and you will see that it shrinks in size when it becomes solid. The lower temperature means that the atoms move about more slowly inside the mercury, and pull tighter together and more closely-packed as the liquid freezes. That's how liquids are expected to behave. But water – that fantastic, versatile liquid found in such abundance on our beloved planet – doesn't play by those rules.

Instead, water gets less dense on freezing: ice is less dense than water. Freeze a glass of water and its volume (the water, not the glass) will increase! This is all to do with the chemistry of the water molecules (the little particles of water, many millions of which make up each droplet). Water is made of oxygen and hydrogen, with one oxygen atom bonded to two hydrogen atoms in each water molecule. This is a happy circumstance, because each hydrogen atom contains (as we saw in Chapter 7) only one electron. To bond with the oxygen, it shares this negatively-charged electron with the oxygen atom, which has space for two extra electrons (hence it bonds with two hydrogen atoms). That means that the positive charge – the proton – at the centre of each hydrogen atom is left unshielded by any electrons. Meanwhile, oxygen is very 'electro-negative', which means that it hugs its electrons particularly close to its nucleus and it ends up with a slightly negative charge because of the two electrons it is 'sharing' (in practice, hogging) with the hydrogen atoms. Why is this important? Because it means that the slightly positive hydrogen atoms in one water molecule become attractive to the slightly negative oxygen atoms in other molecules (remember, opposite charges attract), and adjacent water molecules are therefore pulled together in what is known as a 'hydrogen bond'.

This sort of bond doesn't exist in most other liquids. It means that when water freezes and these hydrogen bonds solidify, frozen water (ice) has an unusually open crystal structure, with big gaps between the molecules, and this is what gives the ice its unusually low density. Without hydrogen bonding, water would freeze at a lower temperature and get denser on freezing, not less dense. This is important for life because it means that, ice being less dense than water, ponds and lakes freeze from the top downwards, with the ice floating to the top rather than sinking to the bottom. During the many Ice Ages that Earth has experienced over hundreds of millions of years – caused by interacting cycles of variation in its tilt and orbit around the Sun called 'Milankovitch cycles' – this allowed life to survive in watery places beneath the ice, where otherwise it would have frozen to extinction. This was especially important during the 'snowball Earth' era about 800 million years ago, when Earth was entirely covered in ice but life somehow survived! This marvellous chemical fact is an example of how not only Earth itself but also the very laws of nature are well-suited to the existence of life on this planet.

The other evidence we have for evolution having led to life as we know it today comes from our examination of living organisms and their DNA, which carries with it the ghosts of past individuals that each organism is descended from. As I've mentioned before, DNA is the genetic 'code' that tells our cells how to function, and is instrumental to our design when we are conceived and begin to grow within our mother's womb. But a lot of DNA is shared between different species – we share nearly all our human DNA with other primates, and most of it with all other mammals, despite being very different indeed in appearance from, say, a rat. That's because a lot of the DNA in our genetic makeup doesn't actually do anything at all: it sits there as a (largely) unused relic from a time when it was active in some distant ancestor.

Yet even this non-functional DNA has some uses, not least for those interested in the history of life. By tracing back how much DNA each species shares in common with other species, it is possible to work out when those species last must have shared a common ancestor, and to some extent what that ancestor was like, forming a sort of family tree of life containing various branches where different species diverge from one another by adopting sufficiently different genetic code. Again, that this should be possible would have amazed our forebears, even the discoverer of Natural Selection Charles Darwin himself, who lived long before genes and DNA were ever even hypothesised.

Combining the fossil record with this living history gives us a relatively clear picture of life's evolution, and provides quite incontrovertible evidence that we are where we are because of evolution. And, let's face it, doesn't that make much more intuitive sense than the alternative anyway? Everything we know of in the universe and in our own day-to-day lives has to be created somehow by a tangible physical process, with clear cause and effect (unless, of course, you're talking about the quantum realm, which we'll get onto in the next Chapter). It would be very surprising indeed if living beings – so very complex as they are – just popped into existence fully-formed, without developing gradually in a series of smaller and much more explicable and probable steps.

As if that wasn't enough, evolution itself has left behind a few clues to show us without doubt that this is how life was made: apparent 'mistakes' that one would never build into an organism on purpose, but which make perfect sense in the context of the evolutionary story. One famous example is that of the human eye, in which the nerves that connect each of the light-sensitive cells on the back of the eye travel to the brain in front of these cells, not behind them as would make more sense if we were designing the eye ourselves. The nerves therefore have to be transparent, so as not to block the incoming light from reaching the light-sensitive cells, and they reach the brain through a hole in the back of the eye which gives rise to a blind spot in our vision (you don't notice it because you have two eyes and the brain automatically compensates for it). It seems mad, but it can be explained by considering the eye's evolution: over many, many generations, cells under evolutionary pressure became sensitive to light, and only gradually developed into a fully-fledged retina in an eye capable of focussing that light to form a sharp image. The back-to-front nature of the eye's information-carrying nerves – a nature shared by the eyes of all vertebrate animals and thus possessed by their common ancestor too – arose as part of this gradual, organic development. The eye was never designed as a distinct organ. It developed gradually through evolution. In deep-sea non-vertebrate animals, incidentally, it developed differently: their eyes don't have nerves on the wrong side of the retina!

The feats that life has achieved on Earth are incredible. So far as we know, throughout all the rest of the universe – and certainly throughout most of it – life is entirely absent, as it cannot survive in empty space, the hot plasma of stars or the barren, frigid conditions of most planets, asteroids and moons. Yet on our little planet orbiting our average-sized star, life has clung on aggressively for four billion years – a staggering amount of time if you think about it, equivalent to living 1000 years 1000 times, then doing the whole thing 1000 times over! It's survived asteroid impacts, volcanic super-eruptions that have frozen the whole globe, and the volatile chemistry of an ever-changing planet. There have been at least six mass-extinctions that we know about (one of them the Mass Oxygenation Event, three of them the ones the dinosaurs experienced, plus two more in between) but even these have left a sizeable proportion of life intact. Life is like an unstoppable machine, reaching into every corner of the globe and altering the environment of the air, land and sea unrecognisably to suit its own survival and development.

We are part of this story of life; hominins like modern humans evolved from primate ancestors over the last two million years or so. There will soon be eight billion human beings on Earth, each of them far more complex than almost anything else in the universe. There are countless billions more conscious, thinking beings – all kinds of animal life – alongside them. And even this is peanuts compared to the countless billions of plants and trillions of bacteria with which the Earth is teeming on its every surface and even in the clouds and deep underground. Earth is an island completely and irrevocably infected with life, in the midst of a vast, empty void. And it's all powered by evolution by Natural Selection. That is a true miracle indeed!

9

The Quantum Realm

Everything we see, hear, touch, interact with and know about on a day-to-day basis – and much more besides – is part of what we might refer to as the 'macroscopic' realm. Think of it as anything that's not microscopic or smaller! Most other types of lifeform that we are aware of live, like us, in that realm. We've known since the 17th century that there are other organisms much smaller than this – so small in fact that we need a microscope to see them. These are known as 'micro-organisms' and include such delights as bacteria and viruses, which larger beings such as ourselves actually depend upon to live – especially to digest our food and recycle our waste – although a small minority of them can cause us harm. They exist in the world of the microscopic.

Yet even these microscopic organisms are themselves made up of atoms, which are much smaller still, and those atoms are mostly empty space because their protons and neutrons and the electrons that orbit them are even smaller still. It's on this unimaginably tiny scale – as many orders of magnitude smaller than you and I as galaxies are bigger than us – that very strange (to us) things start to happen, which we would never see in the macroscopic realm, or even the microscopic. This unimaginably small scale is what we mean when we refer to the 'quantum realm'.

The term 'quantum' is really nothing to be afraid of, exotic as it sounds. It comes from the fact that at the smallest scales, most things appear to be 'quantised' as opposed to 'continuous' – that is, they have to have a very specific value, rather than just taking any number arbitrarily. That's not something we often encounter in the macroscopic realm. Take speed, for example. If I'm driving a car in the macroscopic world, I can in principle go at any speed I like, up to the limit of the car's engine (although of course I should stick to the local speed limit too!). I can go at 30mph, or 20mph, or 27.5mph, or 23.4621mph, or at any speed in between. The more precisely you specify the speed you want me to drive at, the more difficult it is for me to achieve it exactly, but it's still in principle possible for me to drive at any speed up to, say, 120mph.

But this would not be the case if speed were 'quantised'. Quantised speed would mean only a few specific speeds were possible, and nothing in between. For instance, imagine that your car could travel at 10mph, 20mph, 30mph, 40mph and so on in 10mph intervals, but only at those precise speeds. It would be impossible to travel at, say, 25mph. To get from 20 to 30mph, the car wouldn't accelerate gradually: it would have to instantaneously leap, from one speed to the other. One millisecond it's 20mph, the next it's 30mph, with no time in between at all. Wouldn't that be odd? But that's exactly what happens on very, very small scales – in the quantum realm.

Electrons orbiting the nucleus of an atom don't behave like cars or bicycles or people. Electrons have to have a very specific energy – think of it as a 'speed', if you like – one of the 'energy levels' of the atom in question. This means that they can't just orbit at any speed or any distance, like planets around a star. They can only orbit in specific positions. What's more, only two electrons at the most are able to orbit at level 1, closest to the nucleus, and 8 electrons at level 2, further out, with further restrictions on the successive levels further away from the nucleus than this. In the quantum world it's definitely not 'anything goes' – there are very strict rules about what is permitted and what is not. An electron can change energy level instantaneously, by gaining or losing exactly the right amount of energy – no more, no less – provided there is space for it where it's jumping to. Such jumps are called 'quantum leaps', and the term has entered everyday language, indicating a sudden step-change from one thing to another with no intermediate gradation. Often in everyday parlance we're describing a big step-change, but in the quantum realm a 'quantum leap' is the smallest possible change.

We've only known about these quantum effects that go on at the scale of the extremely small for about a century, but to be honest the idea that things might be quantised in this way on the universe's smallest scales wasn't much of a surprise. Think about the car again, accelerating from 20mph to 30mph in our macroscopic world in a gradual manner. Say it goes from 20 to 30 in ten seconds. If the acceleration was constant, then, we could say that it was at 25mph after five seconds. Cut the time in half again, and it would be at 22.5mph after 2.5 seconds, or 21.25mph after 1.25 seconds, or 20.265mph after 0.625 seconds. How long can we keep on doing this? Was the car travelling at 20.000001mph after 0.00001 seconds? Surely, if we slowed footage of the car down sufficiently – and had a very high shutter speed on our film camera – at some point the car's acceleration would cease to be smooth and its speed would increase in distinct jolts as the engine boosted it up. We'd get to a point where the car's speed seemed instantaneously to increase, after all – just not in 10mph jolts!

So, if we look over a small enough time, the car's motion is in fact quantised. The world on a very small scale has to be quantised – the Ancient Greeks knew this. They worked out that matter must ultimately be made of tiny indivisible chunks they called 'atoma' – hence the modern world 'atom', though in fact what we call 'atoms' today are divisible into electrons, protons and neutrons, and protons and neutrons are made of indivisible quarks, which are what we would label 'atoms' if we were really sticking to the spirit of the Greek word. If nature wasn't ultimately composed of discrete chunks, the Greeks realised, everything would have to have an infinite density because there would be no empty space: you could always fit smaller things in the gaps between larger ones.

Furthermore, the Ancient Greeks also proved that motion in the universe is quantised on the smallest scales, not continuous. The proof of this is known as 'Zeno's Paradox' (it was actually one of many that the philosopher Zeno came up with), and it goes something like this. Imagine a hare and a tortoise running a race. Now, the tortoise is much slower than the hare, so to give him a chance he gets a head start. He manages to get a quarter of the way to the finish line before the hare sets off. Now, she can run at twice the speed of the tortoise, so we all know what the result will be: she will overtake the tortoise half way to the finish line, and win.

But now let's slow down the motion, and try to find the point at which the hare catches the tortoise up. Soon enough, she will have run a quarter of the race, reaching the point where he was when she set off. But by then, the tortoise will have moved half this distance again, since he runs at half the speed, so will be another eighth of the way to the finish line by now. By the time the hare has travelled this distance, the tortoise will have moved on again, half the distance the hare has travelled in that time, so will still be a sixteenth of the total distance to the finish line ahead of the hare. Keep on like this, and you will see that the hare never reaches the tortoise, because he will always have moved on a little bit by the time she reaches where he's just been. Yet we all know that the hare does overtake the tortoise! What's going on?

The only solution is to discard our notion that motion is continuous, and can be divided indefinitely in half so that the tortoise always goes half the distance of the hare within a finite time. If instead motion is quantised into little leaps forward, either because the method of propulsion is quantised or because space itself is quantised, there comes a point where the hare can move forward to the next quantum position while the tortoise stays still, stuck at the previous level. If I reframed the story so that the tortoise jumps forward one square on a grid chalked into the ground every time the hare moves forward two squares, there would be no paradox: the hare would overtake the tortoise. Hence, it must be the case that the hare makes two quantum jumps in the time that the tortoise makes one jump, at some tiny spatial scale where there can be no further division of the motion into smaller parts. The hare then overtakes the tortoise, no problem.

Looked at in this light, the quantum realm isn't so remarkable – even the Ancient Greeks knew about it, though they didn't use the word 'quantum' (which actually has a Latin origin, though it wasn't used in this sense until the twentieth century). However, things being quantised is not the strangest feature of this curious realm: far from it! If everything was quantised in such a straightforward manner, things would be simple. But nature isn't simple, it's messy – at least, to our feeble human minds. Take those neat little particles, electrons. These aren't actually very neat at all, but fundamentally fuzzy. That's because their properties can't be adequately described in terms of definite particles like billiard balls or even specks of dust that we experience in the macroscopic world. As well are being particles in one sense, electrons also behave, at the same time, like waves!

Indeed, it would be better to picture the electron not as a point object in orbit around the nucleus, but as a cloud spread out around the nucleus. Its exact position we can't know; we can only know the probability of the electron being in any particular place, and the mathematical curve that describes this probability is the electron's 'wave'. That is to say, the electron is like a wave (think of a water wave) whose crests are at the places of high probability for it to be found there, and whose troughs are at places of low probability. The two electrons in the orbit closest to the nucleus (which I mentioned in Chapter 8) in fact merely have a higher probability of being close to the nucleus than those in the other orbits further out.

The same is true of all 'particles' on the quantum scale – they are all also waves. They have what is called a 'wave function' describing their position. This is also true of photons, the particles that make up a ray of light, which we perceive as if it were a wave. The really odd thing is that if we treat light as a wave it behaves as a wave, whereas if we examine it particle by particle it behaves as a particle. Nobody – not even quantum physicists – really understands this. We just have to accept that whilst 'particle' and 'wave' are good metaphors for objects on the quantum scale, really these objects are something else entirely that we can't really picture. In fact, it turns out that the more we try to pin down any property of a quantum object, the more uncertain all the other properties become – if we look for its position (as if it were a particle), its speed (which depends on its wave nature) becomes more uncertain. Quantum objects are elusive!

Though the existence of the quantum realm is not unexpected, then, many of its features are unlike anything we see in the macroscopic world and, quite frankly, baffling. At the end of the nineteenth century, scientists thought they had the universe all worked out:

given enough information about the state of the universe at the present moment, given enough observations of all its constituent particles, they could – they thought – use a few simple principles to predict exactly what would happen in the future. It was a 'clockwork universe', completely predictable and deterministic, and it was looking very unlikely that there was really any such thing as true randomness or free will.

Then quantum physics was discovered, and everything was thrown up in the air. It turns out that, in the quantum realm, it isn't always possible to predict what is going to happen. Will the photon pass through slit A or slit B when I fire it at a sheet of paper? It's not just very difficult to predict: it's impossible. The outcome isn't determined before the photon sets off. On average, of course, the results are predictable: fire enough photons and half of them will go through slit A and half through slit B, all other things being equal. But for an individual photon, it is impossible to know in advance.

By and large, then, this quantum uncertainty isn't immediately obvious in the everyday macroscopic world: everything we see, hear, touch and know about is made of a very large number of tiny quantum particles put together, and their behaviour averages out to be predictable and understandable. However, the truly random events that occur on the quantum scale can set in motion a chain of larger-scale events that can cause changes in the macroscopic world too. So-called 'quantum fluctuations', tiny changes on the quantum scale that can't be predicted, can grow and grow and give rise to a change in atmospheric pressure that eventually leads to a storm, for example, and that's one reason why it's impossible to predict the weather accurately.

Such a cascading effect is one consequence of 'chaos theory', which states that in a chaotic system – and our atmosphere is a chaotic system – any uncertainty at all in the initial conditions used to produce a forecast (to predict future weather, say) will cause the quality of that forecast to rapidly decline the further into the future you try and predict. Quantum fluctuations mean that no matter how good our observations of the present atmosphere and no matter how powerful our computers, we can never produce a perfect weather forecast. Nor can we predict anything else beyond the very near future with any certainty. Uncertainty (and possibly space for free will) are back on the cards!

Another strange feature of quantum mechanics is what Albert Einstein mockingly labelled 'spooky action at a distance'. He didn't think it was real, it seems so contrary to our everyday understanding of the laws of physics, but experiments have since proven that in this, Einstein was wrong. It is possible, in the quantum realm, for two quantum objects – such as electrons – to become 'entangled' with each other. That means that there is always some property they share that is either the same for both or opposite for each, such that changing that property for one of the entangled pair will also change it for the other one. So, if you measure that property for one of them, you know what it will be for the other. Think of it like a pair of gloves: if one of the pair is observed to be left-handed, you know at once that the other one is right-handed, even if you can't see it or it's been carried away somehow to the other end of the universe. If one glove is 'right', the other is 'left', there's nothing strange about this.

The difference in the quantum world is that properties like this – 'handedness' in this example – are not necessarily already fixed before they are measured. It all comes down to probability once again: a particle might have a probability of fifty percent of being 'right-handed', and one of fifty per cent of being left-handed. Only when the particle is measured does it assume one of the possibilities, and the property becomes fixed – it settles on left-handedness, say. This is very different to the macroscopic world we live in, where (at least as far as we know) things have definite properties, whether or not we are observing or measuring them. If I put the pen with which I am writing this away in a drawer, it remains the same pen with the same properties; it won't suddenly decide to be a pencil, or hover between the two possibilities. A right-handed glove stays a right-handed glove, regardless of whether it's being worn or not.

In the quantum realm, these certainties do not apply. So, if I take two entangled particles, one of which must become 'left' when the other is 'right' and vice-versa but I do not measure which is which, it's not simply that I don't know which is which: this hasn't been determined yet. Both of them are hovering between the possibility of being 'left' and being 'right'. They're each in a 'superposition' of both states. Now, the difficulty comes for Einstein (and everyone used to the macroscopic world) when I use special equipment to separate these two entangled particles, without observing them, and send one of them out to, say, Alpha Centauri (our next-nearest star) and leave the other one on Earth. Then, if I look at the one on Earth and it assumes the property 'right', instantaneously the one in Alpha Centauri will settle on 'left'. If the one on Earth assumes 'left', the one on Alpha Centauri chooses 'right'. The quantum uncertainty is destroyed.

But how did the particle all the way away at Alpha Centauri know that its partner had been observed, and that it must settle on the opposite state? Even light takes four years to travel the distance between the two places, and nothing goes faster than light, so there's no way a message could go from one to the other instantly – Einstein had proven this in his theory of relativity. Yet, because the two particles are entangled, one of them 'knows' the state of the other at all times and places. It's as if they were a married couple who can never ever wear the same colour of socks as one another, to the extent that the moment one of them puts on white socks, their spouse's socks turn black, or if one of them dons black socks, the other's turn white, wherever they are and whatever they are doing. We'd never expect to see anything like this in our everyday world. Somehow, particle A affects particle B without sending a message: 'spooky action at a distance' indeed!

Einstein believed that this couldn't be right: the states that particles A and B would each settle on must have been determined in advance, albeit unknown to the observer who thinks they're truly random. B must know to be 'left', and A to be 'right', when the measurement is made: then there would be no need for spooky means of communication. But subsequent experiments have shown that he was wrong. Exactly how they did so is too complicated for me to explain it here, but you'll have to take my word for it: the states of the two particles aren't determined beforehand; they really do communicate with each other instantaneously. A precious tenet of classical physics – 'locality', which means that entities can only directly affect their local surroundings, and have to send something physical (a beam of light, or some other force-carrier particle, or a homing pigeon) to affect things further away – had been broken. It simply doesn't apply in the quantum realm. Nor, strictly, does 'causality' – the idea that cause comes before effect. No wonder people think that quantum physics is weird!

It's certainly not 'anything goes', though, as I mentioned at the outset of this chapter. This quantum strangeness is confined to the fuzzy world of the very small because (for reasons we don't fully understand) these principles of locality and causality do apply in the macroscopic world, when there are lots of particles interacting with each other and acting on aggregate. Entanglement (in the quantum sense) and superposition of states do not occur in macroscopic objects. 'Spooky action at a distance' notwithstanding, it is still not possible to send a message faster than the speed of light, because the state that an entangled particle collapses into is truly random, so you can't communicate a message via the state of its entangled partner on Alpha Centauri or anywhere else: you can't predict whether particle A will settle on 'left' or 'right' when you observe it, so you can't control and manipulate the entanglement link.

There have been many attempts to draw out philosophical implications from quantum weirdness, especially this idea of particles settling on properties (location, speed, energy, handedness, polarisation) only when they are observed. Observed by whom? Humans? Any conscious form of life? Clearly the fixed, predictable macroscopic universe preceded these. Perhaps any macroscopic object could do the observing? Or any other particle? Or God? We still don't know for sure.

Some physicists have decided that every time a particle in quantum superposition seems to settle on one of two possible states (following such an 'observation'), the universe splits into two copies, identical except for the outcome. So, there would be one universe in which particle A chose 'left' and particle B was 'right', and one universe in which they were the other way round. Given the unimaginable number of quantum particles in the universe, not to mention the number of possible particle states, this would rapidly give rise to a multiverse of near-parallel universes of an incomprehensible size. There's absolutely no hard evidence in favour of this really quite absurd notion whatsoever, though, and I'm not inclined to believe it.

Another possibility is that there's some deeper theory that explains why one state is settled on rather than another when quantum superposition break down, which we just haven't discovered yet or can't ever know. After all, physics is all about asking 'why' and if there's a 'why' you can't answer that usually implies that you need a new theory. Quantum Mechanics is incompatible with General Relativity, Einstein's triumph of a theory about how the universe behaves on the big scales where gravity dominates, so surely one of them must be incomplete? In the few places where they meet – for instance, the centre of a black hole where gravity is extremely strong but the size of the 'singularity' in the centre is exceedingly small – the outcome isn't pretty, and the two theories wildly disagree about the amount of energy contained in empty space (the 'energy density of the vacuum').

The standard interpretation of many physicists (a lot of whom think that it's relativity, not quantum theory, that requires the tweaking) is the so-called 'Copenhagen Interpretation', named after the place where it was first devised. Put simply, this interpretation says that quantum physics is just weird, and we have to deal with it as it is. Perhaps we will never fully understand it – who knows the limits of human comprehension? – but we can at least use it anyway, and lay aside the philosophy for now.

There is one consequence of quantum mechanics that has a very important repercussion for the everyday world of you and I, though: as I touched on earlier, all this quantum uncertainty implies that the universe we live in is not deterministic. In other words, the universe's future is not determined solely by its condition today, the future isn't all mapped out already and there is room for some degree of manoeuvre – which could allow for the existence of 'free will'. Because tiny effects on the quantum level can ripple upwards to the macroscopic scale, those ghostly effects can have tangible consequences. For instance, 'quantum tunnelling' can occur, whereby the uncertainty in a particle's exact energy can allow it to leap over a seemingly impenetrable barrier that would usually require too much energy for it to overcome. This means that otherwise impossible physical reactions and interactions can take place, given the right conditions, and such tunnelling is required by theories in branches of science from astrophysics to chemistry to make sense of what we see.

Thus, although quantum physics doesn't prove that humans and other conscious animals might have free will – because our thoughts could still be influenced solely by predictable, macroscopic physical factors, making our sense of free choice illusory – it can at least leave open the possibility that we do, a possibility that 'classical' physics had all but ruled out. It could just be that, deep within our minds, there exist quantum 'superpositions of states' that we genuinely can control. Zoom in far enough to the physical stuff of the universe, and we find that it is a much more mysterious, complicated, unpredictable and deliciously fascinating place than anyone might have guessed at the turn of the twentieth century.

Part Three

Growing into God

10

God in Creation

In the previous three chapters, I've told you a story. I could call it The Story – or at least, my humble take on it. It's the story of the universe, the story of humanity, the story of everything, briefly told. It's a true story, backed up by evidence gathered by the well-established means of theory and experiment. Human minds and physical equipment have worked together to figure out the details of the key characters, the settings and the plot. And what I want you to draw from this holistic picture of the universe from the very big right down to the very small is that it's a story of evolution. None of it popped into existence out of nowhere; all of it evolved, in all its beauty and complexity and its amazing ability to give rise to intelligent life, from a single point source into the whole of creation.

That infinitely small, infinitely dense point before the Big Bang didn't have wrapped up in itself already the whole future of the cosmos: the spooky properties of very small quantum objects tell us that there was much room for uncertainty regarding exactly what would spring from that rapidly-expanding proto-universe. But the way that it ended up happening was this. First, fundamental forces formed that would go on to be essential to how the universe functions: gravity would gently control the birth and death of massive stars and their encircling planets, the strong force would allow stable atoms to form, electromagnetism would permit energy to travel from one place to another. All are essential to a complex universe, and all have just the right properties to make it work.

Next, a seething sea of particles crystallised out that could interact through these forces. Then, suddenly, 300,000 years after the Big Bang, this sea became transparent to photons: there was light! And it's still ricocheting round the universe to this day. After that the matter clumped into galaxies and the first stars began to form, evolving out of clouds of primitive gas, and themselves exploded – according to the laws of physics that somehow arose in this universe – giving rise to more stars, moons and planets. Not long after its formation, on one of those planets at least, life had its genesis: first invisible single-celled organisms like bacteria, then creatures of the deep sea, the plants and land-based animals, then birds and mammals and human beings, all developing according to the principle of Natural Selection over thousands and millions of years. From a tiny quantum-scale entity to a fully-fledged cosmos containing conscious, rational, thinking human beings able to reflect on all this, in about 14 billion years. The universe somehow evolved to be able to contemplate itself, in the form of us – collections of matter that have minds. Amazing!

Scientists know this today through experiment and observation, using the very best modern technology to make their equipment. But people have also known all this for thousands of years, through a miraculous revelation we know as the Book of Genesis. Let's compare the scientific account of the universe's evolution I've just described above with the story of creation we've already encountered in the first book of the Bible. Here it is, based on the King James Version with the language updated a little for a modern-day audience:

"In the beginning, God created the universe.
And the universe was without form, and void, and
darkness was upon the face of the deep.

"And the Spirit of God moved within this deep void.
And God said, 'let there be light': and there was light.
And God saw the light, that it was good, and God
divided the light from the darkness. And God called the
light Day and the dark Night. And this darkness and
light were the first epoch.

"And God said, let there be physical material in the
midst of the void, and let it divide the void into denser
and less-dense spaces (galaxies). And God made this
physical stuff and drew it into shapes within the void.
And God called this physical matter the heavens (the
cosmos). And there was darkness and light in the second
epoch.

"And God said, 'let there be a particular coagulation of
physical matter, gathered from the dust that I've made,
forming Earth'. And he gathered water together to form

seas, and he saw that it was good. And God said, 'let the Earth develop grass and seed-bearing herbs and trees of all kinds', and it was so, and God saw that it was good. And day and night passed in this third epoch.

"And God said, 'let there be lights in the sky to mark signs, seasons and years', and it was so: the Sun ruled the day and the Moon the night; he'd made the stars too. And time passed in this fourth epoch.

"And God said, 'let living creatures be brought forth from the sea, then fly in the air'. And God created great whales and sea creatures, then birds of every kind, and God saw that it was good. And God blessed them, saying, 'be fruitful and multiply and fill the seas and lands'. And day and night passed in this fifth epoch.

"And God said, 'let the Earth give rise to all kinds of living creatures on the land – all amphibians and mammals and reptiles and crawling insects.' And it happened. And God saw that it was good. And he said, 'let mankind develop, being like me – capable of thought and creativity – and let them gain control over all the fish, birds, insects and Earth itself'. And he made humans, male and female, and blest them too, and told them they could eat any of the plants he'd made. And God saw that all that he had made was very good, and there ended the sixth epoch."

The resemblance is uncanny. It's true, I've shortened the passage slightly for clarity in this translation and I've used some modern terminology you won't find in most Bibles, but I invite you to look at any translation of the opening chapter of Genesis and you'll see that the resemblance to the modern scientific account is not my invention. I've translated the Hebrew word for 'period of time', which is often misleadingly rendered as 'day' (which it can indeed mean in some contexts) into the less-specific 'epoch' to give a truer sense of the indefinite meaning of the word. Very few people believe that the world was made by God in six Earth days, and that's not what the Hebrew original says either: it says something more akin to 'epochs' to use a modern term in English.

By and large, the order of events and their nature as recounted in Genesis is exactly what science shows us, except that the author of Genesis seems to imply that the Moon formed after the first life on Earth, which is almost certainly not true – though we do know that the Moon formed later than the original Earth through a collision with another planet. This notwithstanding, everything is there: the formless void of space in the beginning, the formation of matter, the sudden switching on of light when the universe became transparent, the coalition of galaxies, the condensing of stars and planets, the evolution of plants and sea-creatures then land animals, with mankind a late arrival.

Crucially, Genesis doesn't at all give a 'creationist' account of everything being suddenly created in a single week (about 4004 BC according to the creationists) as if out of nothing. It gives an account of evolution, from Big Bang to human being, with one thing leading to another. Notice that Genesis doesn't even say, 'God made light, then God made the Sun, then God made plants and animals' and so on. It says, 'God said, "let there be light" and there was light', or 'God said, "let the Earth give rise to all kinds of living creatures."' It's not God putting things into the universe as if dropping them out of the sky. It's a story of God willing them to come to being, organically, springing forth in a progression of evolution. God didn't turn on the lights, he set things up so that they could come on themselves at the right time. Yes, he wanted everything described in Genesis to happen, and his guidance was undoubtedly upon it, but it was one thing leading to another – not sudden creation – that gave rise to everything we see. Genesis is a story of evolution, just like the scientific account.

So how did the author of Genesis know all this? Did he or she have access to telescopes and particle colliders? Had they access to fossil records of DNA transcribers? Did they work it all out using mathematical equations? No. And yet, somehow, they knew: the people of Israel, the chosen nation of God, knew. There's only one way in which they could possibly know. They must have been told by God himself. If you're looking for evidence that God not only exists and set in motion the creation of the universe but also interacts with his creation and reveals the truth about himself to mankind, you need look no further.

And it doesn't stop there. The more modern science tells us about the details of creation, the more and more miraculous it seems that we could be here at all, and the more and more evident is God's hand in having set all this up. Our universe isn't one in which things just pop into existence out of nothing – or if they do, they're very, very small and only exist for a tiny, tiny amount of time (but I won't go into the details of such 'quantum fluctuations' here). The whole of physics is about asking 'why?' because there is always an answer – in the real, physical world. Everything always has a cause, a reason, an origin. So what about the universe itself? Why does it exist at all? Would it break its own conservation laws in order to pop into existence out of nowhere?

Some people will tell you that the universe has always been there, expanding and contracting in a never-ending cycle. But that's no satisfactory explanation for what put it there in the first place, carrying on such a cycle. Other people will talk about the beginning of the universe being the beginning of time itself (which indeed it was), as though because there was no time before the universe in which God could create it, he can't have done so, and as if time is the one thing that doesn't have a cause: it just starts. That doesn't sound a very good explanation either. Anyway, God is by definition outside time: he uniquely doesn't need to exist 'before' the start of time to create it. That's the whole point. Or, they'll point to the fact that in certain senses the universe might 'balance out to zero': for every particle of matter there's a particle of so-called 'anti-matter' and all the positive energy of the universe is balanced out by the same amount of 'negative energy' which we can't ordinarily detect or experience. Well, that might well be so, but just because things balance to zero, that doesn't mean they don't need a cause. If I dig a hole and form a mound, the hole and the mound may add up to nothing but they don't come out of nowhere; somebody still has to do the digging!

Sometimes, I don't like thinking about the question of the origin of everything, because it makes me very frightened, if I'm honest, to think that nothing should – scientifically speaking – exist at all. Everything has to have a cause so how can anything be? But then I remember that God is both inside and outside time and space; God isn't restricted by the laws of our universe. After all, God made it. It's the only logical explanation. You see, I believe in evolution, not creationism: in cause and effect, not magical conjuring acts. I don't believe in a universe that just appeared out of nothing any more than I believe in horoscopes and pixies and chocolate teapots in orbit about the Sun. The idea that time and space just came out of nowhere to me smacks of creationism; the notion that it has 'always been there' makes no sense. I personally don't go in for any of that superstitious nonsense. I believe in what I have evidence for. I believe in God.

If the miracle of creation existing at all isn't enough to tell you there must be something beyond this physical universe, let's look at some of the many, many miracles within it that provide hard evidence of the presence of God. A miracle is to my mind something that works out well, even when in all probability it shouldn't. Science can explain a lot in our universe, but there are a lot of questions that it simply cannot answer, things that it has no explanation for. We encountered many miracles in chapters 7, 8 and 9, though perhaps you didn't recognise them all as such because they have been discovered by science. Yet all of them are unlikely occurrences without which our existence – and our understanding of the universe – would be impossible.

We have the miracle of electromagnetic radiation – light – that can travel unobscured through space and show us the state of the universe billions of years ago and lightyears away, allowing us to shape our picture of the cosmos and prove Genesis right. We have the miracle of exactly the right state of carbon existing so that there are any elements at all heavier than helium. We have the miracle of the fundamental forces of nature being in just the right balance that stable worlds can form. We have the miracle that there exists a planet where the conditions are just perfect for life to evolve, and that the laws of physics allow this to occur somewhere in the universe, and the miracle that life is so resilient it can survive asteroid impacts and a 'snowball Earth'. We have the miracle that fossils can be preserved to tell us the story of evolution, and that we've been able to invent technologies capable of reading DNA – it's almost as if God wants us to be able to know the story of our origins!

The fact is that there are countless extraordinary things about the universe that make our lives possible, and allow humans to know as much as we do about physics and biology. Think about all the amazing technologies of today, from aeroplanes to motor-cars to touch-screen computers. None of these things existed before humans invented them; it wasn't a given that they would be possible to make. Yet, somehow, the universe is such that all these technologies that we find very useful – and which may prove crucial, used rightly, to the happy existence of a world with 10 billion people on it – are possible. God has given humans room to create! The universe also happens to be non-deterministic, featuring quantum uncertainties that are not pre-determined outcomes. This gives space for its inhabitants – including us – to have free will. When we look at the inner workings of the universe, through quantum and particle physics, we are looking at the work of God. This is how he made the universe (or even the multiverse!) to be, with all the properties necessary that it might give rise to life that could know and love Him.

The signs of God's presence and his love for us are everywhere, if you just open your eyes and look for them. The whole universe is within and part of God, and his life runs throughout its entirety. He speaks to us in the miracles of everyday life, miracles that might seem small and inconsequential to onlookers but can mean a great deal to the person to whom they occur. He's there in the miracle of the rain holding off just long enough to get the job done; in the miracle of missing the bus – and thereby meeting an old friend you'd otherwise not have crossed paths with; in the miracle of being in the right place at the right time to meet your future spouse, or to hear about that job that was just right for you to do. These sorts of 'coincidences' happen to us all the time, when we somehow know that it was 'meant to be', and even many atheists and agnostics admit to having that feeling.

To give you a trivial example from my own experience, there was a time when towards the end of a holiday in Ireland, my family's hire car broke down. My brother – not a theist – was due to leave early by plane, and consequently missed his scheduled flight. However, it just so happened that on that particular Saturday (and no other Saturdays) there was also a plane from a different nearby airport to the same destination, which brought him to London two hours late. Arriving at the music festival he was travelling for, he found his friends getting out of a different taxi at exactly the same time, having been delayed by precisely the same amount for completely different reasons. What are the chances of that? Meanwhile, coming back to the UK by train a little while later, I was unexpectedly delayed half an hour and yet arrived at my destination station at precisely the same time as the person fetching me, full of apologies for being late, quite by chance. I hadn't contacted them (I don't have a mobile phone): it was what you might call a coincidence. Yet I drew from it the certain feeling that, for all that things can seem to be going wrong, it all works out according to God's plan: we are in his hands.

Indeed, people of faith such as myself put ourselves in God's hands for guidance throughout all we do, and when countless such occurrences as this occur as a result, it all begins to look like divine arrangement. With our eyes open to see it, we recognise that everything happens for a reason. And how could this not be? After all, God is everywhere and everything is in him: of course he can set things up to show us signs and wonders, whether they're amazing spectacles of nature or just a series of ordinary things happening in an extraordinary manner. Of course he wants to reassure us of his presence in our everyday lives.

Some people are perturbed by this notion of God's always being present, as if he were some sort of all-seeing security camera in the sky watching our every move, in front of whom one mustn't do anything wrong for fear of being punished. But God is not some scary Big Brother surveillance tyrant. The reason is that we ourselves, remember, are part of him, and he is part of us. He's not watching us and judging us from afar; he knows our thoughts and feelings as well as our deeds, and he understands why we do things. He knows and loves us so intimately that he understands why we make mistakes. He knows our temptations and our weaknesses, and although he sees our sins he therefore also forgives us them.

God is always with us like the best friend we could ever want to have – even if it doesn't always feel like it, in this fallen world. This is evident to anyone who takes the time to make a heartfelt prayer or to reflect upon the true nature of the world around us. In it, we endure many pains and sufferings, whatever our religion and spiritual practice, and life can seem very hard. But God is there, not just as a creator, but as a constant companion – brother, sister, mother, father, best friend all in one. We know this to be true because of the billions of people who have had – and still have – an active relationship with him. They are not idiots, they are not deluded; they are very unlikely to be suffering from a form of mass hallucination. They – the people of faith in One God throughout the world – believe and trust in Him because of the evidence they have seen with their own eyes and heard with their own ears. They have felt in their own hearts his presence and his love.

Because God wants us to love him with a free and willing heart, he doesn't give us from birth a fully-fledged understanding of him and realisation of his presence. God values no more than we do a false 'love' that involves grudgingly serving another out of cold duty or desire for something in return, or out of fear and control. Would you really like someone to say kind and flattering words to you, knowing that they were only doing so because they were frightened you might punish them? I certainly wouldn't. Nor does God. He wants us to choose to believe in him, and to love him.

We are not all born into belief naturally, therefore. We all have a choice: to believe and trust in the creator of the universe, who loves us and will guide and protect us if we let him; or to believe and trust in ourselves, trying to live a good life from our own point of view and gratifying, at best, only ourselves. Usually, when we make up our own way of living life we fail to stick to our self-imposed principles and beat ourselves up about it, or else give up on the whole thing and give in to every temptation. Even if we could stick to rules of life that we've just invented for ourselves, what would be the benefit when we die and are no longer able to judge ourselves? How can we know that the 'moral code' we've made up was really to the benefit of others, or the best way of living?

If we are to make the most of our lives, and to be sure of what we're doing, we therefore need to learn to turn away from self-centredness and to acknowledge the presence, power and providence of God. If we serve him who is everlasting and in all things, we also serve ourselves and all other conscious beings which are part of him and loved by him. We must do this, though, at the expense of not gratifying our own selfish desires all the time. This is no hard sacrifice; it is a liberation, a realisation of our true selves. It is a growing up, from our childish selfishness and wilful mistakes; a growing into God.

We grow into an understanding of God like we grow into our adult clothes, casting off our childish rags of self-centredness to put on the garments of Truth, to use a Biblical metaphor. But we also grow 'into' God in that we become more and more like him as we do so: more and more loving, generous, content, and in awe at the wonder of creation. We become more and more eager to create the fruits of love, faith, joy and peace that God delights in the most.

Growing into God needn't involve any strict creed or dogma. To grow in understanding and appreciation of our creator you don't have to enter any organised religion or adopt strict rules that somebody else has drawn up governing every aspect of your life. It's secular powers that have time and again wanted people to do that. God makes us all different but equally valuable, and to adopt a formal religion is for some an expression of love that they value, whereas for others religious traditions are not so useful or necessary. All you really have to do is set your heart on God and show him your love within your heart, to give your life to him. Then he will guide you into what he wants you to do. Once you do this, the onward road isn't difficult; it's the easiest, most liberating thing in the world: to accept his love, guidance and protection, and to no longer have to worry about 'getting in right' for yourself.

It is unfortunate that this is not how many of the most powerful (and therefore the most visible) people of 'faith' have portrayed belief in God down the centuries. Indeed, it has often been said that power corrupts, and achieving a position of power – in the church or in a secular authority – may often have required acting in a selfish, ambitious and downright ungodly way. From the Pharisees of Jesus' day claiming you had to be 'ritually clean' to be loved by God and getting so concerned with the Sabbath that they refused for good deeds to be done on that day of the week, to extreme puritans of the Reformation era claiming that only the elect few could enter into heaven to the exclusion of everyone else, to terrorists blaspheming God's name by murdering His own children under the guise of doing His will, all sorts of people have told lies about God.

They have set him out to be a tyrant, a slave-driver, a control freak elitist who insists you do everything his way, or pay the price. That's really because they want to play tyrant, slave-master and despot; they want to be the elite and have things done their way, and they want to treat God as any other false idol and use him as an excuse to serve their own ends. Such abuses of God's name are the very epitome of idolatry and sin: setting up yourself as a god instead of worshiping the true God. They've got absolutely nothing to do with Him. For Christians, Jesus Christ is the living incarnation of the true God, and God's nature is best revealed in him. He was humble, generous, loving, self-sacrificing and a friend to everyone. He knew what was right and wrong and stood up for good against evil, not afraid to disagree with powerful forces. He defended the poor and the despised. He was certainly no tyrant imposing his will: he didn't even use his power to save himself when arrested, tried and crucified, and he didn't force anyone to do anything.

If God wanted to be a tyrant, he'd have made us to be robots in a deterministic universe. Clearly, he did not. God wants us to have independence of thought, and to worship him in whatever way suits our true selves. Jesus tells the Christian, 'come to me all you that are heavy laden... for my yoke is easy and my burden is light.' Believing in God is no hardship: it is a release from the burdens that the spotlight of the public eye, those interested in their own power, and we ourselves so often place on us. If we trust in God, we don't need to worry about any of these authorities, we only need to act in a way that is pleasing to Him, and loving to everyone.

Nor does God make it difficult to understand His love for us. All the universe is His creation, and he exists outside both time and space, able to know the whole history of the universe all at once. Therefore, he fills the universe with metaphors that display something of his nature and the truth of his feelings towards us. Take the stars with which he populates the blackness of space. Few if any of these host intelligent beings like us. Yet he has made them to shine for us, that we might look up beyond our own world and its cares, and remember that there is so much beyond our own lives, so small yet so important to him that he made this whole cosmos for us! The cares of today need not worry us, as he is so much bigger than them, bigger even than the vastness of space. The darkness is not endless: the stars twinkle on, the same yesterday and today and throughout all the generations. Indeed, astronomers now realise that even the darkest patch of night sky contains countless galaxies that we can see with our best space telescopes.

Take also the day and night, the patterns derived from living on a world that rotates. These are a metaphor for the condition of our own souls: we may walk in the darkness of suffering for a time, and not see the way to go, with only a few hopes to keep us going like little stars in the night sky. Sometimes even these are clouded over and everything seems hopeless. But the dawn always breaks, and likewise God's love will always break upon us and he will make things well again. He assures us of this through many of the prophets in the Bible. Even when we die, this is not a disaster: we return to 'heaven' to be fully with him. We must never lose hope of the dawn, no matter how dark the night; no matter how difficult the problems that face us and our world.

Another metaphor that God employs is that of parenthood. To all humans – along with nearly all other animals – he gives both a mother and a father, who are there to nurture, care for, educate and protect their children (if they do the role well). Those who lose their father and mother at a young age will, if humanity responds to this tragedy in a loving way, hopefully be given a guardian to take their place. In these relationships we get an idea of the relationship God has with us. He is a mother who gives birth to us, feeds us, teaches us right and wrong if we will listen, and on whom our whole existence depends. He is a father who corrects us, protects us, and yet gives us the freedom to go out and explore the world for ourselves as any father should. No father holds his child's hand every moment of every day to protect them from ever getting hurt, or else the child will never learn to live their own life and will feel held back. So it is with God as our parent. He gives us freedom to run into trouble, but he always steps in to help us when we call on him in need.

God likewise knows what it is like to be a child. He knows what it is to be frightened, sad, tempted, and frail. Christians believe that in the form of Jesus Christ he demonstrated this intense empathy that he has for his children. God gives us all the stages of life, from youth to old age, to give us all a picture of the spectrum of his feelings towards us. We are, after all, 'made in his image' according to Genesis. The seasons are another example, a symbol of God's continuing replenishment of the Earth. The despair of winter and death is not the end, for out of winter always springs summer, even if summer must fall back to winter again. By this, God shows us that his universe is not a place of stasis: it is about continual creation, evolution, death and rebirth and renewal. The very process of growing in wisdom, learning to see God's signs in the world around us, has its metaphor in blossom gradually growing into fruit. That's what growing into God is like: it isn't instant, but it's well worth the patience and effort it entails. I could go on; there are many more metaphors all around us.

To recognise this fundamental truth is to see God's presence in everything. This is part of the process of growing into God that will enable us all to become the beings that we were made to be: each a child of God, in a loving relationship with him. All of us get distracted from this truth sometimes, lost in the cares of the day-to-day world, but people with faith in God are released from these cares whenever they recall it. It is the source of all the purpose and meaning in their lives. That's why we practise faith; that's why we choose to be religious.

If you think about it, most of the things that human beings do are not very lasting, and have little lasting purpose. In the language of the King James Bible (the book of Proverbs), 'vanity of vanities: all is vanity'. Things that seem important at the time so often pass away and are forgotten. What shall we eat tonight? What clothes should I put on today? Within a few weeks we'll have forgotten what we ate and what we wore. As the grass shrinks away in winter, so many of the things we spend so much of our lives thinking about quickly disappear. There are all sorts of people doing all sorts of things – businesses are set up, people spend a lot of time and effort marketing them, advertising, drawing in custom and making a profit. But soon enough that money is spent, more custom must be sought, and in the fullness of time even the biggest of businesses will close.

That's not to say that businesses are bad things: many of them provide something that makes people's lives better. But to suggest that the business is an ends in itself, that doing things and making money is the purpose of life, is absurd. Those things are only good in that they provide a means of living happy, healthy and fulfilled lives in relationship with one another and with God. Likewise, the buildings we construct will eventually fall, the books we write – including this one – and even the symphonies great composers compose will one day be read or heard no more, lost and forgotten. Even the scientific knowledge we accumulate is but a temporary precious store. Again, that doesn't mean that writing books or playing music or doing science is a waste of time – far from it. But what is the importance of any of them when we die? And what happens to all the goods that we gather?

The point is that there's no use doing any of these things for their own sake, but rather for the joy that they generate. That's what's treasured by God. Anything, then, that doesn't give rise to joy and love really is a waste of time. The purpose of life lies in lasting treasure, stored up by the one who does not die – God. Through all the transitory things that we do, the important thing is to generate what he loves, and feels, and remembers for ever: faith, love and joy, every day in all we do. This is the essence of good religion, guiding our whole lives. This is growing into God.

11

Thirsting for Truth

'Wherever you see Truth,' said the great sixteenth-century Christian humanist philosopher Erasmus, 'look upon it as Christianity'. These profound words ring true to this day, and I mention them here by way of introduction to what will be the theme of this penultimate chapter: that there is no distinction between the search for Truth – be it scientific, moral or theological – and faith in God. It's a point we've touched upon numerous times throughout the rest of this book, but it's one worth emphasising for its own sake, as well as in order to counter two pervading myths about theism that I haven't yet mentioned. It may be that either or both of these two quandaries are still an obstacle to your understanding of God.

So far, I've explored with you many sources of evidence for the presence of God and about God. We looked at the evidence of personal relationships with God, and at the many scriptures that people have written in response to these relationships – especially the Old and New Testaments of the Bible. We saw that these texts, correctly interpreted as sources of moral truth, were never intended to be necessarily historically accurate in many cases, but that they are not inconsistent about the nature of God: that he is a loving, generous and forgiving creator who made us that we might be in relationship with him. In later chapters, I took you through the story of the creation of the universe and living beings, and we saw how all this is testament to the creative power of God who set everything in motion – and still guides his creation – so that people like you and I would come into existence and be capable of acknowledging him. I explained how Growing into God properly involves seeing his presence in everything, even within ourselves.

The evidence that God is there, listening to and responding to us, is utterly incontrovertible. Without God, the universe is without form and void: it is senseless, meaningless, and impossible. Meanwhile, God's presence is felt by many millions of people every day. I know it. Everyone who truly opens their heart to God knows it. And I want you to know it too, because it is the truth.

There are, though, people who would try to convince you otherwise. I've written this book partly as a direct response to some of the arguments that those people make, and the misconceptions that lead them to believe that there is no God. There are two 'counter-arguments' that some people will use to put forward the quite astounding notion that, in spite of the universe's existence, our existence, and all the interactions of humanity with God through so many millennia down to the present moment, He does not exist. These arguments are first, that human beings are hardwired to see an 'agency' in everything by evolution, such that we might imagine God's presence when he's not there; and second, that perceiving God in nature – in the universe all around us – is nothing more than to invoke a so-called 'God of the gaps' whereby we use God to explain away any gaps in our scientific, purely physical understanding of the world. These are both well-considered and meaningful arguments, which deserve a proper exploration and response, and so I shall deal with each of them in turn here. But neither of them puts any doubt in my mind, having considered all the evidence at my disposal carefully, that God is there and looking out for us all.

Evolution by Natural Selection has imbued us with many characteristics. All of them have been useful, at some time or another, for our survival as a species, giving our ancestors a reproductive advantage over others without those characteristics. Many such characteristics have to do with avoiding threats that would otherwise kill us. For that reason we, like many other animals, evolved to be on the watch for predators – 'agents' we might call them – such as lions, snakes and tigers that might try to hunt us. Individuals of our species whose DNA made them too fearless, who didn't read into a rustle in the bushes the sound of an approaching danger, would most likely be killed before they had the chance to pass on these cocky genes to any children. Likewise, those whose DNA made them especially flighty wouldn't do very well in life because they would never be able to get on with anything – like foraging for food, making tools or having sex – if they took fright at the slightest breath of wind.

Thus, humans had to have the right balance of confidence and fear to be able to survive in a dangerous world and pass on their genes – and more than this, they had to be able to recognise potential predators as 'agents' whose behaviour they couldn't necessarily predict. An 'agent' here means a being capable of thought, persistence and clever tricks performed with a particular aim in mind. An agent like a lion or a bear can be contrasted with something that lacks agency, such as a stone or a tree or a river – these might still be dangerous, but only by accident: they can't set out to harm you, they don't have 'purpose' in what they do. The lion's purpose is to eat you, so she might pursue you and creep up on you. You have to recognise the lion's agency if you are to avert being killed.

Once we see agency in lions and snakes, however, it's inevitable that we will start to see it in things that aren't agents as well. Sometimes our ancestors would have heard the bushes rustle and run, when it was actually just the wind. Eventually, the wind comes to seem to have 'rustled' the bushes as if it were doing so on purpose, like the lion. Indeed, we're so attuned to the idea of sounds and signs of danger being caused by agents that some people will see a shadow, or feel a breath of wind, in a dark night in a churchyard and think it's a ghost whose purpose is to scare them or kill them – just like a natural predator might. In actual fact, of course, it's probably (unless it's a bird) just the wind or a shadow, or something else that doesn't have agency: these things don't have any 'purpose' in and of themselves, they can't think and act for themselves.

Now, the trouble is that looking for agency in everything seems to have led our ancestors (and indeed our contemporaries) to invent many of the false gods we met in Chapter 1. That's because people started thinking that the wind must have an agency of its own, and assumed it was controlled by the 'wind god'; that the sky had agency of its own, and dreamt up the 'sky god'; and so on. In this sense, 'god' is really just another name for 'agent' – and indeed, as we saw, people and other animals who have agency were sometimes worshipped as gods too.

If those things all have agency, they can choose what they do – the wind chooses to blow, the sky chooses to rain – and people develop practices of worshiping the 'sky god' or 'wind god' and even sacrificing animals or even children to appease them, in order to encourage rain at the right time and so on. Common sense leads them astray. Common sense tells them that because last year they sacrificed to the rain god and it rained at the right time, the same sacrifice has to be made this year in order for it to rain. Common sense, acting on a natural propensity to read agency into everything, leads people astray and they start performing all sorts of rituals to appease the gods of the earth, sea and sky that do not really exist. They're all just in the imagination.

Is a belief in God likewise just 'in the imagination'? Is it a mere superstition like not walking on the cracks in the pavement because someone at some point had the idea that doing so was linked to bad luck? Is the link between praying to God and good fortune a similar red herring? Or is it even a more sinister superstition invented to control people, like Father

Christmas being invented as a judgemental agent who lives at the North Pole in order to make children behave themselves? Is seeing God's agency in all the world around us just another misapplication of common sense, contrary to what a properly thought-through scientific approach would tell us?

It won't surprise you that my answer to all those questions is, in a word, no. In fact, belief in the One God isn't common sense at all, and it runs quite contrary to the polytheistic tendency to read non-existent agencies into everything. Perhaps God intended us to evolve the tendency to perceive agency in everything so that we could, indeed, come to see the truth of His agency throughout the whole universe. But our natural tendency is instead to see many gods, not a single God, at work. After all, there are many lions, tigers and snakes, all with their own agency – and many human beings. The natural inclination, therefore, is to see everything from rocks and rivers to cars and computers as having their individual minds. Most of us do it all the time, even in our modern post-enlightenment technological world. Who of us hasn't found ourselves reprimanding a computer for being too slow or doing the wrong thing, or cursing the rock on which we stub our toe? That's natural.

To believe that none of these things is an agent in itself, but all are part of the one true God – that's something different. Seeing the One God in everything, and perceiving his action in coincidences and miracles of everyday life, isn't at all like imagining gods into rivers and rocks. What's more, plenty of believers have plenty of evidence to show that a real agency – God – is active in their lives and that their prayers are heard. Take the story I heard of a heroin addict whose mother miles away, unbeknown to her, prayed for God to save her from her addiction and felt one night that her prayer had at last been answered – and who was healed of her addiction that very same night. Take the examples I gave in Chapter 10; take countless other modern-day little miracles. If these things happened to believers just once in a while, they could be counted as coincidences. But when they happen time and time again to people who pray – like me and many others – they cannot be anything other than signs, sent to us from the One God who is the single agency in whom the whole universe exists.

I'm not trying to suggest that our prayers are always answered straight away. Prayer is many things, but it is not a means of making requests or demands of God, expecting him to do whatever we selfishly ask. Prayer is a conversation with God, a coming into his presence, and a coming into an understanding of his will and what he will make happen. In prayer we bare our feelings before God and let him know what we would wish might happen; I might pray for a sick person, asking for their recovery, but that doesn't mean that I expect them to instantly recover. Sometimes, I feel in my heart that God has healed this person, and they do recover. But if God speaks into my heart instead that it is time for them to die, I no longer pray that they will recover, but that they will rest in peace. Prayer is God's way of reassuring us: a means of being reconciled to what he knows is best.

Science has disproved many things that are common sense, from the Sun orbiting the Earth to heavier objects falling faster than lighter ones under gravity (all objects in fact fall with the same acceleration). But belief in God is not mere common sense, and science is not a threat to this belief, but can only enhance it. Science is an important part of the Truth that Erasmus defines as Christianity, a religion that is not concerned with deceit or falsehood (though undoubtedly some have abused it to speak false things in God's name wrongly), but with truth, wisdom and understanding. I believe that all religions inspired by God are 'Christian' insofar as they involve faith in the Truth, which is what Christ came to reveal. Science is therefore a Christian vocation, just as much as is studying scriptures or prayer: it involves discovering the hidden secrets of God's universe and making them plain. That's why Christian teaching never contradicts science. Clinging to Creationism is not Christianity!

Nor is Christian morality common sense – far from it! The common sense morality that we evolved as humans – still practiced by ancient tribes that survive today in parts of the world – is one of tribalism and enlightened self-interest. Essentially, this morality holds that it is good to do good to other members of your own tribe, because they will do good to you in return and protect you, and because by working together you can all do better than you could do alone. A good spear-maker in partnership with a good hunter makes for a good catch of meat that neither could obtain alone. But people from other tribes are a different matter. They are enemies, competitors, and dangerous. If they are come upon in need, they will not be helped; they may even be killed.

This tendency to help people like ourselves and to be suspicious of those who are not like us is, unfortunately, hard-wired into humanity, and is still very prevalent today. Think of all the inequality and xenophobia our world suffers: the rich storing up wealth and ignoring the poor because they are of a 'lower class'; immigrants from other countries or people with different coloured skin being discriminated against – these all arise from our innate 'default' morality of tribalism. There are ways that it can be overcome, though – through education, mixing with other people and coming to recognise everyone as being part of our own tribe. Or, through channelling tribal urges into harmless competition instead, such as by supporting a football team.

Christian morality, and Jewish and Muslim morality for that matter, is very different to this. Christ taught his followers to 'love your enemies, and do good to those who persecute you'. He taught the parable of the Good Samaritan, a very famous story in which the Samaritan, who would be looked down upon as part of a rival, inferior tribe by Christ's Judean audience, turns out to be the hero – the only person willing to go out of his way to help an injured man on a dangerous road. The message is one of universal love, one of not allowing tribal barriers to distance you from the love of others.

Christ even allowed himself to be killed by the Romans – another, quite different tribe who had invaded and conquered Judea – so that he might show God's love for everyone through the resurrection. Indeed, Christ put love, not self-interest, at the heart of all he did and taught his disciples to do the same. And what is 'love'? 'Greater love has no man than this,' he said, 'than to lay down one's own life for others'.

Where does this monotheistic morality spring from? Evolutionarily, it would be disastrous: turn your other cheek to the wild tiger that's hunting you or the rival that picks a fight and you'll soon be dead; fail to stand up for your own needs and you'll lose out and starve. It doesn't come automatically to us, and that's because God delights most of all in our choosing to love him and one another, as a conscious choice. That's why he's had to send so many prophets to the Jews, the Qur'an to the Muslims and Christ himself to the Christians to show and tell us how to live. God's way is not the easiest way, but it is by far the best. It is self-sacrificial. And it's a long way from tribal or pagan morality.

If God's agency is real and all-encompassing, you might ask, and if he so loves all the beings that he has made, why does he allow us to suffer so much pain? The reason is simple: all pain has, at root, a human origin, not a divine one. I don't mean all physical pain: all animals experience that. But physical pain is only really bad because of the emotional pain that it usually gives rise to, and all emotional pain comes from humans. It arises ultimately either from greed or from fear. Our own greed turns us away from God so that we make bad decisions, and we suffer – and it causes harm to others when we take things for ourselves at their expense. Others' greed, meanwhile, hurts us when they steal from us, exploit us, poison us or damage our environment. As for fear, our fear causes us worry, anxiety and depression, and can lead us to lash out against others or to hide away from others that might be in need of us. When things go wrong – natural disaster, attack or misfortune – it destroys our resilience.

Both greed and fear have their resolution in returning to God for his guidance and protection. God is not the cause of our pain or our sorrow; it's not his will that we are miserable. Nor is he anything less than all-powerful, as if he couldn't prevent those sorrows. Rather, he allows us to suffer sorrows, for a time, but only so that we might learn to love him all the more. Imagine you're about to enter a wild wood, that could contain all sorts of dangerous things. The keeper of the wood shows you the path, and reassures you that as long as you keep to that path, no harm will come to you, and you'll get safely to the other side. But stray from that path, and you'll run into danger. It's not the keeper who inflicts this danger on you; it's your own choice to turn from the way he's shown you. So it is with God and humanity: we collectively have strayed from the path, into the wild wood of sin, and the ensuing difficulties are of our own cause, not God's. Yet as soon as we call to him for help, he is there, showing us the way back.

When other people cause us pain, we learn to turn to God for healing and for strength to forgive; when we cause pain to others, we learn to turn to him in repentance to be assuaged of our guilt. God does not desire us to be in pain, but rather than just taking it away immediately and coddling us in cotton wool, he lets us experience it and use it as an opportunity to strengthen our love for him. God allows us to sin, to doubt, to mess things up by ignoring him if we choose, precisely because what he loves most of all is our choosing to turn back to him for healing and forgiveness. That is a great encouragement, when we feel all too obviously less than perfect: God didn't want us to be necessarily perfect in the first place!

God created the living universe out of dead nothingness; his work is always to bring good things out of bad. There are always glimpses of his heavenly light to be seen if we look for them, even in the darkest night of despair. Plus, this life of difficulty prepares us all the better for what is to come. What is a lifetime tainted with sorrow, compared to the eternity of joy he promises when we leave this Earthly life and are resurrected from death? Nature contains a metaphor for this too: the rainbow. This most beautiful and awe-inspiring natural phenomenon can only ever come about through the coming together of two factors: sunshine and rain. Likewise, the light of God's love for us is shown most beautifully when it is refracted through the everyday sorrows of our world.

Seeing God's agency in the universe, then, is not just a by-product of evolution. The believers in God – of whom there are billions today, even if not all of them are actively religious – have plenty of evidence for his existence, and plenty of ways in which he is present in their lives. To those who do have daily conversations with God through prayer, his existence is as certain as that of the Sun. Furthermore, it is from this standpoint – of first knowing God's existence within our hearts – that theists then interpret God's presence in the wider universe and look to the nature of his creation and the events that occur within it for signs from God.

That is why no mainstream theist believes in a 'God of the gaps'. This somewhat derisory phrase is used by those who wish to criticise theists to misrepresent most theists' actual beliefs. Such people wish to make out that believers are somehow on constant retreat from science, as if science and religion were somehow at war with one another and as if religion has provenance only over that shrinking corner of reality where science has not yet discovered the Truth. The idea is that before the scientific enlightenment a few hundred years ago, everything in the universe was ascribed by people to God for want of a better explanation. Then, as science revealed more and more about how the universe works, uncovering underlying principles, laws and patterns, there was less and less unexplained that could be put down to God, leaving at the present day just a few 'gaps' where science doesn't have a full explanation. Into those gaps, theists supposedly jump in and claim that God is the missing link. For example, these gaps might include the creation of the universe in the first place, the exact origin of the first life on Earth and the nature of consciousness. After all, science has answered many questions but our understanding of the universe is still far from complete.

Certainly, if one were arguing in favour of theism just for the sake of it, one might seize upon such gaps as evidence that, since there's no other explanation, God must exist! But nobody argues in favour of theism just because they want to win an argument. They do so because they know that God exists, benefit from that knowledge and want others to be able to benefit in the same way. To the theist, everything is made by, and can be explained by, God, whether or not we have also discovered the scientific explanation for it. A gap in the scientific knowledge has nothing to do with the existence of God or not: all that such a gap can illustrate is one of two things. Either that we don't know the explanation for something yet, or that our human minds are too limited to be able to understand the explanation at all.

The only way in which gaps in our knowledge can be used as evidence relating to the question of God's existence and the veracity of Biblical revelation, is that we seem to be able to understand so much! The specifics of the universe (or even multiverse!) are hard to grasp (where exactly did life begin? Why is that particular star that particular size?), but we've done a pretty good job at making sense of the general principles. It's amazing that we've been able to peer down into the quantum realm, see into our own evolutionary origins, and gaze across the cosmos to discover much of the universe's history. If we are indeed 'made in God's image', and he made the universe, it is not surprising that our understanding shows so little sign of hitting a brick wall. If there was no agency behind the universe and it somehow just randomly appeared and evolved (which to me sounds as ridiculous as a pixie suddenly condensing out of the air before my face) we might expect that our understanding could be quite limited. We wouldn't just happen to have sufficient cognitive capacity to understand the universe.

The historical implications of the 'God of the gaps' idea are also troublesome. It downplays the role, in the development of our modern scientific understanding, of numerous theist scientists that lived before the enlightenment – such as all the great minds of the Islamic Golden Age. It also ignores those theists involved in the Enlightenment itself, from Isaac Newton (the inventor of calculus and an unorthodox Christian but certainly a theist) to Blaise Pascal (a Catholic theologian who invented our modern concept of pressure and the vacuum). All of these people were inspired by their belief in God to search for understanding, not hindered by it. They would be shocked by the very notion of a 'conflict' between science and religion.

A realistic picture of God cannot be that of a 'God of the gaps'. God, if he is anything at all, is the God of the whole. God is One, the One in which all other beings have their existence. Our evidence about him doesn't derive from the gaps in the knowledge that we – with our science hats on – have accumulated, and the things that we can't explain. Quite the contrary. Our evidence for God comes from everything: the explicable and the inexplicable, the very small and the gigantic, the particles and the planets, the laws of nature and the miraculous coincidences. God is in the full and lively places, and the quiet and empty ones; he is in the past and the present, with us through the rough and the smooth. Indeed, God is with us in all of it – every twist and turn of our lives – ready to listen to our prayers: both what we speak to him and what we do with our lives. And he loves us all with the deepest love that any of us can imagine.

That is what the evidence of our senses and of our souls tells us: science and theology (which just means the study of God) are really the same thing – an attempt to understand the Truth. There is the temptation for us to get too obsessed with one aspect of the truth for us to explore the whole truth of the universe, which is very dangerous. Looking at science's explanations of the physical universe, we can forget that it all has its being in God and was made by him, and ignore the revelations he's made to us in scripture and in our own hearts. Thinking only about theology, we can get far too bogged down in what theologians and philosophers have said about God, or in the laws presented in scripture as though they were commandments for all time, and forget to enjoy a relationship with God and what he is doing in the here and now. If we are to live – really live – and understand the truth of what the universe is and why we are in it, we need to look at all the evidence, and see God in all his fullness: in creation, in humanity and in our very selves. Therein lies the way not only to knowledge or understanding, but also to wisdom.

12

Faith in the Future

There is, as we have seen through the first eleven chapters of this book, plenty of evidence to prove that God exists. Some of the evidence is scientific and objective, seen in the world around us. Other evidence is more personal and subjective. But you may be wondering at this point, for what reason should you or I not only believe that God is there, but (as most monotheists do) believe *in* God, in a more active sense? Why should we trust him, put our faith in him? Why should we want to live our whole lives in a way that is pleasing to him, and give him our allegiance? What's in it for us?

First and most obviously, of course, there's the fact that God made us. He is immortal and outside of time, whereas we are mortal and have lives that sooner or later run out (at least in this world). No matter how well-known any of us is today, there will come a time when nobody alive can remember us, or when nobody is alive to remember anything at all. But God remembers us. So, then, he's the one we should want to please, so that he remembers us fondly. We were made by him, and he is the one who gives our lives purpose. Why did he make us? Scripture gives us two reasons: because he yearns for a loving relationship with freely-thinking beings, and in order that we might be stewards of his creation, loving one another and cherishing all that he has made. That is our purpose in life: nothing more complicated, or onerous!

If I fashioned a tool – a hacksaw, say – and if hacksaws could talk, I wouldn't expect my hacksaw to turn around and say 'I'm not sawing any wood for you. Why should I? I think I'll go and take a beach holiday in Bermuda instead.' The hacksaw has no business taking holidays of any kind, or doing anything else than what I want it to do, because I made it with a purpose in mind. I might have made it badly and it might not do the job well, but its purpose remains to saw wood – unless I choose to repurpose it. So, if God made us, albeit via the messy mechanism of evolution, he gets to decide what our purpose is. If a tool I'd made refused to do what I wanted it to I would be outraged. I might seek to destroy and replace it, and quite justifiably. Isn't God justified to do the same, if we decide to take a holiday from doing the not exactly unreasonable work of loving each other that he wants us to do?

Actually, though, God isn't like this. He isn't like me. God is more loving, forgiving, more merciful than I could ever be, because God is perfect in his love. He wouldn't get angry with the hacksaw, or destroy it, disappointed though he might be with its upstart attitude. It's the same with us: it's our duty to serve God, but he's not going to punish us if we don't. God wants the beings that he's made not just to obey him because they're afraid of him, but to love him, because obedience without love is nothing more than slavery. It is evident that to God, slavery is detestable, an 'abomination' to use the Biblical language. Another reason to put faith in God, then, is that serving him is not slavery but freedom. Faith in God, who loves us, frees us from enslavement to other powers, which usually don't. Doing God's will always leads to the best outcome for everyone, even if it seems difficult some of the time.

People have risked their reputations; looked foolish the eyes of other people; been mocked in public; been stripped of their wealth and possessions, family and friends; been imprisoned, abused and even killed, for the sake of doing what is good and right or speaking the truth – all in God's service, who loves truth and hates deception. Not everyone is called to make these painful sacrifices, which would not be necessary at all if everyone loved and served God, but nor is life easy for anyone who devotes themselves to God. Then again, life in a fallen world is seldom ever easy – whether you believe in God or not. At least if you have faith in God you know that he will make your sacrifices and struggles worth something – he will remember the love and the joy that you've shown and known, and treasure these for ever, whilst the sorrow and the pain he promises to wipe away. At least you'll know that you have pleased your maker, and that by our striving to do good the best outcome will ultimately come about.

The service of God may sometimes be physically, emotionally and spiritually demanding – it cannot be denied. That's because we and our ancestors have made a mess of our relationships with one another and with God, and have failed in our stewardship of his world, giving rise to a lot of difficult problems and conflicts. But the everlasting spiritual reward of our devotion to God is beyond comparison. If you risk your own life to do a good deed for another, the love, thankfulness and joy that you thereby create is an everlasting jewel. It's what life in this universe is all about! And you can do many such deeds if you trust in God and allow Him to lead you. And why not? This present life is, after all, so short and transitory: we're here today, and gone tomorrow, and what use then is a lifetime's worth of material riches? Faith in God, on the other hand, gives lasting pleasure.

Incidentally, you may at this point be wondering about the alternative to the everlasting pleasure associated with 'heaven': the idea of 'hell', which I haven't mentioned before now. Traditionally, hell has been seen as an eternal torment, presided over by the character of Satan or 'the Devil', an idea with which the Church has sometimes quite wrongly tried to frighten people into belief in God. Fear of this kind has nothing to do with godliness, for it is derived from falsehood rather than truth. Pretence of belief on the basis of fear rather than love is worth very little to God.

The truth is that Holy Scripture tells us very little about hell beyond the 'wailing and gnashing of teeth' that Christ warns us about in Matthew's Gospel. Satan is a very shadowy figure, popping up in Genesis, Revelation and in the book of Job but mostly absent from the rest of the Bible, and as we've already seen (back in Chapter 1), he is not a real 'god' as such. He is, rather, a character used in Biblical stories under various names (the 'beast' in Revelation for instance) that illustrates the way in which we can seem almost to be possessed by somebody else when the pains, pleasures and blind alleys of the world lead us to act selfishly and to do very evil deeds. 'What's got into you?' is an expression commonly used of somebody who is misbehaving. If we are true to our truest selves – doing what we really desire in the depths of our hearts – we are not sinful. But, alas, too often we do what we know to be wrong against our own better will and judgement. A metaphor for this is that it's Satan tempting us to do wrong.

Another name for Satan is 'the accuser', and the Satan character to some extent embodies a representation of the memory of all the bad things we have done when we are 'possessed by an evil spirit' in this way (understand that we are not literally possessed, but figuratively, by the desire to do wrong). Just as God remembers all the good, the love and the joy that we have created in life when we have been true to ourselves, so does the Satan character remember everything that is bad. Yet the character of Satan, the Book of Revelation tells us, is ultimately defeated by Christ and his accusations are cancelled. In other words, there is no Satan: our bad deeds are forgotten and discarded by God. That's what it means for Satan to be defeated. And the destruction of the memory of our bad deeds is precisely what makes them so bad in the first place: pain, sorrow and cruelty are worthless, wasted time, wasted life, wasted grief and anguish where we could have been doing good.

What, then, is hell? Hell is being confronted with the bad things that we have done. Hell is facing the shame and humiliation of all the hurtful words we've spoken and all the cruel and selfish deeds we've committed – often in secret – being brought to light, out in the open, for all to see. It is having God himself look upon our ugly nakedness, which ever since the metaphorical story of Adam and Eve we have been desperate to cover up from him. Hell is that most bitter and uncomfortable emotion: remorse. How desperate we feel when we have wronged someone and earned their disdain, disapproval and rebuttal, to make it right again and un-blemish our relationship! How we wish we could turn back time and undo what we have done!

The concept of hell is simply that if we do not repent of our sins – that is to say, feel remorse and ask God for forgiveness for what we have done – in life before we die, we will have to go through all the 'wailing and gnashing of teeth' of remorse after death. We will feel all the remorse that we ought to feel, at least until God disposes of all those sorry episodes for good. If our life has only been bad, there will be nothing worth remembering in it – nothing left of us to dwell with him in the heaven of eternal pleasure. A character like Satan, all evil and not at all good, would therefore be utterly forgotten. But of course, none of us is wholly bad, and so a part of us all will always be loved and treasured by God. At least, this is my picture of heaven and hell, and I believe it on the basis of all that God has revealed to us in Holy Scripture, the emotions that we feel on Earth, and the revelation that comes to all who ask for it through prayer.

In light of all this, then, we might as well give our allegiance to God now, and not wait to be full of remorse after death! Not because of fear of punishment, but through love of God who saves us from our fear and our sinfulness. But faith in God doesn't mean pleasure only in some future life after death, and suffering in the here and now – far from it! God has no desire for us, his children, to suffer. Faith also makes our world a much better and richer place in this life. If you have faith in God, as I explained above, you are freed from the enslavement of fear. Knowing that you're doing his will, you know that he will protect you and guide you, and that even if you fall into mishap he will make all things right again – the whole universe is God's after all! So then, what have you to be afraid of? What have you to be ashamed of? Faith in God gives us courage, and strengthens us to fight all those battles that need to be fought today. Battles against injustice, against slavery, against the greedy destruction of our planet, against inequality: all are fought all the more vehemently with faith than without it.

Those with faith in God do not abandon this world to its troubles because they are focussed only on the world to come. That's not what any of the Holy Scriptures I know of – and certainly not the example of Jesus Christ – teach us to do. Faith in God means that we are able to bring his light of love, wisdom and healing into a world darkened by sorrow and the scars of despair. Prayer is about action, not just words. It involves working to heal the sick and the frail whom we ask God to heal and care for, it involves challenging the corrupt powers – be they rulers, governments or corporations – that are polluting the world that we pray to God to preserve and exploiting the people we pray to God to protect. Prayer only works if we put our actions where our words are and demonstrate our willingness to improve the world. That's what makes faith so powerful.

With faith in God, we can solve the problem of world poverty: we can share the resources he has given us fairly, knowing that he will have provided enough for everyone to be well-nourished so long as we feed according to need, not greed. With our faith in God we can avert the problem of climate change, by sacrificing unimportant luxuries and excessive lifestyles for the benefit of others, knowing that God will provide for us what we need personally and bring about a happy and prosperous world for everyone. Living more simply, with a lighter footprint, is a means of reducing the harm we cause the planet as individuals but also a prayer to God to save us from the environmental catastrophe precipitated by many modern ways of living. It's also essential if we are to live up to our purpose to steward his planet and delight in his creation.

Theists know that the whole world is in God's hands. He can restore the ecosystems he made and rebalance the global thermostat he set, through whatever means he chooses. But that's no excuse for sitting back and doing nothing. What kind of stewardship is that? God will help us if we show our love for him: if we show our willingness for change and repent of our selfishness, if we stop needlessly pumping out such quantities of pollutants to produce unnecessary luxuries and treating other animals we are supposed to cherish as worthless slaves. He may use natural means to restore his world, or may show us the way and use human means to effect change: God works in all sorts of ways in answer to our prayers. But if we all just give up on him and one another and destroy our own planet, ignoring his warnings, he may well let us drive ourselves to extinction.

With faith in God, we can also solve the everyday problems of our lives: even if we are sick, or stressed, or sorrowful or hurt by others, or others we love are hurting, we can talk to God and trust in God for help. He is a great source of hope, healing and resilience. He reminds us that life is still worth living, and that he loves us whatever happens; he encourages us to carry on. We perceive him in the everyday miracles of life, in the people around us and in the deepest intentions of our hearts, and that is a steadfast source of comfort and inspiration.

Indeed, at this time of unprecedented crisis, facing climatic change, ocean poisoning, deforestation, inequality and plastic pollution like never before, the world needs faith in God more than ever. It is not that the problems of the world or our personal lives suddenly disappear when we put our trust in God, nor that we should become complacent and leave things up to him to sort out. On the contrary, true faith equips us, through the strength God gives us, to go out and change the world for the better. That's because we know that we matter to him individually, that he cares about our problems and feels them with us, that he witnesses our efforts to make things better, takes them as prayers and magnifies and perfects them. I'm not trying to argue here that solving the world's problems is impossible without faith or immediate with it, but I am saying that faith makes it a lot easier for us to start. And goodness knows we need to start!

Nor does faith lead us to turn our backs on science, as I hope this book has demonstrated. On the contrary, the more we know about God's universe and the physical and biological principles that govern it, the more amazing it becomes and the more fully we can appreciate God's love for us. After all, if he created all this vast universe – so much bigger than the ancient Israelites could have imagined when they wrote the psalms and sung his praise – how much the more incredible that he cares about little you and I! It's God who enables us to explore his creation and understanding, who imparts wisdom to us through which we are able to do good, who wants us to use our rational minds and employ them in healing the world.

God gives us science and technology, and though we must be careful not to misuse them to abuse his world and its creatures, to reject them entirely would be to stupidly spurn his gift to our own detriment. The person of faith doesn't just wait around for God to cure them and make everything better, rejecting the help of modern medicines and technologies. As it says in Ecclesiasticus, 'the doctor's skill comes from the Most High... the Lord has created medicines... the Lord has imparted knowledge to people, that by their use of his marvels he may win their praise'. If you are sick, pray for healing by all means, but be sure to accept it when it comes in the form of a well-trained doctor as much as when it comes by a miracle cure. Both are from God, even if the doctor doesn't know it. It's not a question of trusting either God's power or human expertise when we need help: God works through people, and lends us his power.

Without faith in God who sees everything, knows me through and through and loves me for who I truly am, I might be tempted to despair at the dire state of the world, and do little or nothing to try to change it. After all, without faith in God, who's to say we won't very soon be destroyed by nuclear apocalypse, runaway climate change or some other catastrophe? As one little man in a world of billions, what difference would my small actions make? Is there any point in sorting my recycling, choosing not to use aeroplanes and sticking to more local attractions, turning down the thermostat and eating sustainable food if everyone else just carries on regardless all around me? Without faith, it would seem mad and fruitless to do this, especially if the world could end tomorrow.

But it's my faith that tells me that the world won't end tomorrow. With faith, I know that God sees my actions, my small sacrifices, my little attempts not to be a burden but a blessing to my planet and its people, and he treats them as a prayer: a prayer that things will get better. And I know that Jesus taught that prayer can move mountains, for 'with God, nothing is impossible' (Mark 10, verse 27). My faith magnifies all that is good in me, so that I can see it as part of a larger, much stronger whole: the unity that is the One God. I know that God will guide me and all people of faith – true faith – and that together we will create a world that is fruitful in love and joy, a world of God's children, grown up into God. That's the sort of world I want to see. And it will come, with faith.

So where does that leave each of us? With our many temperaments, personalities, gifts and limitations, we are all children of God. He calls to every one of us, as a mother or father calls his children individually and longs to share a relationship with each of them. Our lives are a working out of this relationship with God, becoming the person he means each one of us to be. We are all unique, all called to live out a life of fulfilment in different ways and contexts, which is what makes humanity such a precious and wonderful creation. You can do good, and play a part in changing the world for the better. Your life is full of value, full of purpose, and can be full of joy, even if you don't know it yet. And it all starts with just a little faith, to begin entering into your true self – to start growing into God.